TEETERING

TEETERING

Why So Many Live On A Financial Tightrope and What To Do About It

KEN REES

RADIUS BOOK GROUP

NEW YORK

Radius Book Group
A Division of Diversion Publishing Corp.
New York, NY
www.RadiusBookGroup.com

For more information, email info@radiusbookgroup.com.

First edition: March 2021
Hardcover ISBN: 978-1-63576-740-7
Trade Paperback ISBN: 978-1-63576-800-8
eBook ISBN: 978-1-63576-741-4

Library of Congress Control Number: 2020913232

Manufactured in the United States of America

10   9   8   7   6   5   4   3   2   1

Cover design by Tom Lau
Interior design by Neuwirth & Associates, Inc.

For Jeanne (and sometimes Isabel)

CONTENTS

FOREWORD

When I created Black Entertainment Television, I did so because I saw an opportunity to provide consumers with programming content that was not available on existing cable channels. I believed then, as I do now, that you can make a difference and create significant value by reaching out to consumers in industries where they have been underserved or ignored.

Teetering gives a voice to some of the most underserved and misunderstood Americans today. They are the ones who have been left behind by the constant upheavals of the global economy or who struggle to overcome the impact of generations of systemic discrimination. Financial security has become increasingly difficult to maintain and is no longer a guaranteed part of the American Dream. And the COVID-19 pandemic has put people even further behind and at risk.

The need for change in this country and the opportunity to make a difference has never been greater. The first and arguably most important step in this process is listening to and understanding these frustrated and unappreciated Americans.

Their needs resonate with me because I grew up in a family of ten kids with working-class parents. Our family understood what living from paycheck to paycheck meant.

When there was a problem with the car, if you didn't have $200 for the mechanic, you hitched a ride to work, and if something happened to the heat in the winter and you couldn't afford the money to fix it, you were cold. Honest and hard-working Americans shouldn't have to make these difficult choices.

Ken Rees has spent the past twenty years serving millions of financially challenged Americans and has a unique perspective forged from experience and empathy. As an innovator, he has launched many product and service offerings—some that were wildly successful and others that weren't—and these have provided him with the insights that make *Teetering* so important.

It won't be enough to simply wring our hands and bemoan the new economic realities facing so many Americans today. We need to make real change at both the governmental level and in the private sector.

While I believe that our legislators and regulators often act with good intentions, sometimes the most dangerous law of all is the law of unintended consequences. Most credible studies on alternative financial services products have reached the same conclusion: Regulation that eliminates consumer choice has been ineffective at best and at worst harmed and restricted financial access for millions of Americans.

I urge regulators, consumer groups, and business leaders to work together to find a proper balance between too much regulation and too little. While I firmly believe consumers deserve to be protected, we can't let perfect be the enemy of the good.

Nor have banks and financial services providers stepped up to this challenge. Many Americans have grown weary and no longer trust a system full of confusing rules, hidden fees, and lack of flexibility. And they have every right to be frustrated when banks sell them complicated and overpriced products with fees they don't expect or understand. Transparency should be the principle that guides us all.

However, I also firmly believe that financial providers deserve to make a reasonable profit, assuming that they offer products that are easily understood and cost-efficient. I am convinced that traditional banks, as well as new innovators, can become part of the economic solution by providing struggling Americans with access to quality financial services. This will generate growth for those who recognize the opportunity while contributing to the overall economic prosperity and individual financial security of the people in this country.

Teetering provides real-life stories and insights into the pressures that push so many people off of their financial "tightrope," as well as the ways they heroically manage their lives and support their families in these increasingly unstable times.

I urge all of us to listen closely and be a part of making a difference in the most important challenge of our era—making the American dream attainable for every American.

Robert L. Johnson
Founder and Former Chairman of Black Entertainment Television
and Founder and Chairman of The RLJ Companies

INTRODUCTION

I'm in an industry people love to hate.

I make money providing financial services to the people banks don't want.

So why should you read this book? Because the rapid growth of my industry is the result of dramatic changes that have eroded the financial stability of half of this country. Over the past two decades, I've had a front-row seat to the changing outlook of so many Americans, and I've listened carefully to their stories.

Anyone concerned about the economic problems facing this country needs to hear these stories to understand why so many Americans are struggling, and why they so often make what seem like poor financial decisions. It probably won't be what you think.

The Aha Moment in the Bank Lobby

Go ahead, hate my industry. I'm not all that fond of it myself. I certainly never thought I'd end up in such a controversial business.

I was raised in Palo Alto, California, a child of the sixties and seventies, by Stanford professor parents. I studied math at college, worked as a software designer, then earned my MBA from the University of Chicago. After graduating, I worked for a management consulting firm, focusing on information technology strategy and business process reengineering in the financial services industry.

I never had excessive worries about money. I expected that savings would naturally build as I rose in my career and my earnings kept pace. I had confidence in my ability to achieve my financial goals and figured that if I worked hard, it would pay off. Isn't that how it works for everyone?

I am embarrassed to admit that early in my adult life, I never gave any real thought to those who might be struggling with their finances or to those who had been pushed out of the traditional banking system. People who weren't like me weren't on my radar. Until one day, they were.

It was the mid-1990s and I was working on a consulting engagement at a large bank to improve branch productivity. The goal of the engagement: accomplish more with the same (or fewer) staff.

As I met with different branch employees, a term came across their lips that puzzled me: "lobby trash."

Lobby trash?

I didn't see any papers strewn about. The floor was clean. So were the windows. It was a perfectly ordinary scene of an utterly unremarkable bank lobby, with people waiting patiently in orderly lines.

So I asked, "Where is this 'lobby trash'?"

The branch manager pointed to one of the lines. The people in that line, she explained, were a drain on the bank's time and attention.

They were there to cash checks written to them by the bank's customers. Unlike others, who deposited their checks in their own checking accounts and waited several days for the checks to clear and for the money to become available, these people needed their money right away. And they were willing to show up at the branch and stand in line to get it.

"I have no products for these people who come to cash checks, other than trying to get them to bank with us, which they never do," the manager said.

To the branch manager, they were annoyances, at best. To me, they were something very different. I saw people who literally went the extra mile to make sure they had cash in hand for their immediate needs. I saw people who braved an unwelcoming space to get cash a day or two sooner. I saw a handful of people who likely represented a lot more people. People who faced disdain from the financial services establishment.

As I watched the line in the lobby slowly inch forward, I wondered what it would take to design a better way to serve people who were pushed outside the mainstream of financial services. This was before the advent of smartphones. The notion of a "bank in your pocket" was science fiction. I can't claim that I figured that out on the spot, but I did realize that one success factor for a new type of financial service was right in front of me—an unmet need.

At the time, I had tunnel vision. I saw only a business opportunity. I thought that perhaps innovative technology could make a transformative difference in the lives of this so-called "lobby trash."

My Evolution Serving "Lobby Trash"

A while after my aha moment, I founded a company to test my new ideas. We developed and deployed advanced check cashing units in convenience stores and grocery stores across the country. As opposed to the long lines and bulletproof glass in traditional check cashing establishments, our technology gave retailers a convenient, fast, and dignified way to serve their customers' needs. And since we allowed customers to instantly deposit the proceeds of the check on a prepaid debit card with no fee, check cashing was now more safe and secure for vulnerable Americans. Plus, convenience stores have better hours than banks; no skipping work to cash a check.

The idea took off, and after just a couple of years, GE Consumer Finance acquired the company for more than ten times revenue.

Next, I was asked to take the reins of an early-stage online payday loan company. At the time, I still viewed customers with less-than-stellar credit scores as an interesting business opportunity. It was not really something close to my personal experience. As far as I knew, I didn't actually have any family or friends who had ever taken short-term, high-cost loans to tide them over.

And again, I was wrong. I was telling my family about my new job and my sister Beth, to my surprise, said she had taken out a payday loan to buy college textbooks. She felt fine about it. She knew it was an expensive option, but it was worth it to her to get the cash when she needed it.

That was my second aha moment. People whom I knew and respected—well-educated people—could make a rational decision to take out a payday loan.

This new perspective stoked my ambition for this business. I wanted to find new ways to better serve people like Beth. I hoped to use technology to improve on what was good about payday loans—the speed and ease of getting needed cash—while doing it at lower cost.

We started asking customers about their rationale for taking out short-term loans. They knew it was expensive, but that wasn't their biggest concern. It turned out that most of them would rather have more time to repay their loan—even if it costs more in overall charges and fees—than face the nearly impossible hurdle of paying back the entire loan on their next payday. Almost everybody preferred a loan with flexibility over a cheaper loan. Extra time was worth the money.

That insight showed me that cost is not the only factor in customers' decisions. They need power over their cash flow. Control and flexibility over repayments is an overriding priority.

To learn more about our customers, I founded a research institute called the Center for the New Middle Class. The findings from that group helped us evolve our product offerings and are the source of much of the original research in this book.

I moved the company away from traditional payday loans toward longer-term, lower-rate credit products using data and technology. We provided credit to millions of consumers with damaged credit scores and saved them billions of dollars over what they would have spent on payday loans. Major venture capital firms backed us. It took some trial and error, but eventually we took that company, Elevate, public on the New York Stock Exchange.

None of this redeemed me at corporate networking events or cocktail parties. When people hear about the industry I'm in, their eyebrows go up and their noses wrinkle. It's not a 'politically correct' industry. Nor has my contrarian perspective endeared me to my industry peers. I was hissed at an industry conference where I spoke about the problems with traditional payday loans and urged innovation and lower rates.

Even though Fortune 500 companies like Walmart were created to serve Middle America, the daily financial tensions driving the growth of my industry are not well understood by most business leaders, consumer groups, investors, think-tankers, politicians, academics, and media. These well-meaning influencers typically have limited contact with "average" Americans and still tend to think of people without savings as either victims of corporate greed or simply lazy and undisciplined.

I started writing this book to introduce people to the half of America that struggle daily with financial stability—I call them Tightropers. My goal was to provide a deeper understanding of their financial pressures and real-world options to be able to improve their financial stability, which will eventually help us all.

It was an exciting time in my life as I was preparing to hand off the first draft of the manuscript of this book to my editors. I had recently founded a new financial technology start-up to provide even better credit solutions for Americans and things were going more smoothly than I could have imagined. The incredible team I assembled had launched the product in just a few months and we were starting to serve customers with what we felt was the fastest, most hassle-free, and most responsible loan product of its type. I couldn't have been more optimistic about the future.

Then came March 19, 2020. From my office in San Francisco, I listened to the mayor, London Breed, announce the country's first "shelter-in-place" order that would shut the city down for months.

In an instant, my book about Tightropers started to seem much closer to home than ever before. Like business owners across the country, I worried about whether I could continue to provide steady paychecks for my employees and how I would weather the oncoming economic storm that I knew would cause the credit and equity markets to collapse.

As Warren Buffet famously declared, "only when the tide goes out do you discover who's been swimming naked." Like millions of other people who felt they were "stable," I suddenly became aware that my financial safety net was getting seriously frayed.

The truth is that the overwhelming majority of Americans are only a few financial setbacks from becoming a Tightroper. As a country—as business leaders, innovators, policymakers, and concerned Americans—we need to recognize that financial instability has become the overriding economic and societal issue of the twenty-first century. If we don't find solutions quickly, we will face an unprecedented economic meltdown that will tear us apart.

This is when serving the needs of underserved Americans stopped being just a business opportunity and became a mission. I hope this book serves as a call to action for all of us to step up and make a difference in the economic lives of the millions of Americans living on a financial tightrope.

SECTION 1

The Rise of Tightropers—
Life Without a Safety Net

1

INSTABILITY—
THE NEW NORMAL IN AMERICA

Nearly half of Americans work hard but can't get ahead financially

- More than 100 million middle-income American adults walk a financial tightrope due to limited savings, income volatility, damaged credit scores, and the impact of unexpected expenses.
- The number of these "Tightropers" has been increasing since the 1950s but accelerated due to the Great Recession, and is now expected to be the majority of Americans as a result of the COVID-19 pandemic.
- Policymakers and business leaders need to listen to the real-world stories of Tightropers to better understand their unique needs and respond to this growing economic crisis.

About 105 million Americans walk a financial tightrope. That's almost half of American adults.

Over the past decades, they have experienced increasing income instability and shrinking savings and earnings. They are no longer being adequately served by traditional banks, leaving them prey to products that can trap them in a cycle of debt. Today, even minor changes in income or unexpected expenses can cause dramatic financial upheavals for a large portion of the US.

The statistics are stark and highlight the frightening levels of financial vulnerability that many Americans face:

- 78% of working Americans say that they are living "paycheck to paycheck" sometimes or always.[1]
- 41% of the country couldn't cover a $400 emergency expense using cash.[2]
- For 55% of Americans, monthly income can fluctuate by 30% or more. This is true for 70% of people between 18 and 24.[3]
- 30% of Americans say that either they or someone close to them endured a significant unexpected expense in the prior year.[4]
- 56% of working Americans save less than $100 per month.[5]
- 54% of Americans have a subprime credit score or no credit score at all and are typically rejected for traditional bank credit.[6]
- There are more payday loan stores than McDonald's.[7]

A year ago, during a booming economy with unemployment at a fifty-year low, it seemed unimaginable that nearly half of middle-income adults lived in danger of tripping into a financial freefall daily. Now, in the aftermath of the COVID-19 pandemic, we all feel far more vulnerable to economic instability.

Even if this bleak picture doesn't describe your personal financial situation, it will still impact your life. The increasing financial frustrations facing vast numbers of Americans are a dangerous trend in our country. If so many in this country are struggling right now, what happens when they reach retirement? The economic changes that created Tightropers are not going away anytime soon. We need to understand and address them.

The Rise of the Tightroper

So what happened to our country? The US used to have a thriving middle class and a strong working class. Both provided job stability and the expectation of savings and future income growth. The vast majority of Americans felt "Safely Stable." Now, Tightropers outnumber the Safely Stable.

CHART 1.1. Percentage of American Adults by Financial Category[8]

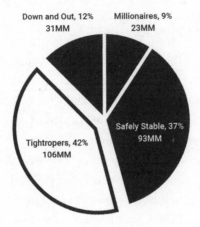

The trend started decades ago. According to data from Trading Economics, US savings rates have dropped approximately 50% from their peak in the 1970s.[9] However, this masks the real gravity of the situation. The bottom 90% of the country as a whole now suffer from *negative* savings.

Shrinking savings rates jeopardize the financial stability of Americans, but this has been compounded by significantly increased fluctuations in monthly income. The volatility in family incomes has roughly doubled over the same period, making it harder than ever to budget and build wealth.

CHART 1.2. US Savings Rates and Income Volatility[10]

	1970s	2000s
Overall Savings Rate	10-15%	5-10%
Bottom 90% Savings Rate	5-10%	-5-0%
Cumulative Growth in Family Income Volatility	25%	100%

These trends tell a very disturbing story. They indicate that the financial life of the average American has changed dramatically since the 1950s and

1960s. In the middle of the last century, Americans could expect to see rising income levels over time, to remain employed at the same company for most of their life, and to build up enough savings to safely and comfortably retire at some point. That is no longer the case.

As of the writing of this book, most of the country has seen no meaningful income growth for decades, and real wages (i.e., wages adjusted for inflation) have actually shrunk since 2009 for the bottom 80% of the country. Rising income volatility has made it hard to save for emergencies and even harder to save for retirement.

Meanwhile, deep shifts in the economy have disrupted millions of jobs. Large swaths of the country are being left behind or find themselves under-skilled for the new jobs that are being created. Even if you study for the right job at the right time, twenty years later you may discover that you have the wrong job at the wrong time. Sure, you can retrain, relocate, and get rehired, but you may have to repeat the cycle in another few years. Disruption might be stimulating for the economy overall, but it is draining for the individuals who are disrupted.

To make matters worse, the Great Recession decimated the savings of large numbers of Baby Boomers and Gen Xers. According to research from the Federal Reserve, the bottom half of all US households, as measured by wealth, have only recently regained the wealth lost in the 2007–2009 recession and still have 32% less wealth (adjusted for inflation) than in 2003.[11]

The financial prospects of Millennials and Gen Zers, meanwhile, have been crippled by skyrocketing student debt and housing costs. The combined impact of these issues across all generations has accelerated the hollowing out of the middle class that began decades ago.

And that doesn't include the effect of the COVID-19 pandemic, which essentially shut down the global economy for months and decimated the financial prospects for entire industries overnight. The full impact on savings and jobs won't be understood for years, but it can be expected that the majority of Americans will become Tightropers as a result.

We cannot achieve many of our commonly held national goals if we do not also dismantle the barriers to Tightropers' financial progress. Stable communities, resources for children's education, a ready and smart workforce, a thriving entrepreneurial economy, self-sufficient retirements—all of this cannot be the American reality if nearly half of us devote most of our attention, energy, and resources to just staying afloat.

What caused this situation? There are lots of theories:

- Rising income inequality caused by out of control capitalism[12]
- The failure of progressive social programs[13]
- The decline in union membership and influence[14]
- The lingering impact of the Great Recession[15]
- The withering of traditional religious values[16]
- The impact of technology-driven industry disruption[17]
- Excessive consumer spending influenced by the media[18]
- The rise of the "gig" economy[19]
- Federal Reserve market meddling[20]
- Climate change[21]

All of these theories are intriguing, and some may even be accurate, but it doesn't really matter. Tightropers are here to stay, and we can't wish them away in the hopes of "Making America Stable Again."

Other books have covered this terrain before. This book differs from others in that it doesn't simply lament the economic inequities in our society or attempt to eradicate them with unrealistic and unaffordable policy suggestions. Tightropers are the new mainstream in this country. Whether we like it or not, financial instability is a fact of contemporary life and is expected to increase, not magically disappear. Tightropers need an improved safety net as well as new tools and techniques to help recover faster from financial setbacks. This book will attempt to provide a framework for how the government and the private sector can make a difference.

This is not a book that views its subject as victims. As you will learn, Tightropers are characterized by resilience, responsibility, and resourcefulness—core American values that keep them optimistic about their ability to manage and ultimately succeed. Nor are they necessarily heroes. Like all of us, Tightropers have made financial mistakes in their lives and are clear-eyed about what they might have done differently. The difference between Tightropers and people with deeper pockets is that, for them, the repercussions of a financial setback are far more serious and can linger for years.

Who are these people? Counter to the misconceptions of many, the Tightropers I have served over the years look like—and very much are—average Americans. In nearly every demographic category, millions of Americans walk a never-ending financial tightrope. That tightrope is the precarious balance between managing day to day financial realities and trying to save for the future.

Tightropers are high school graduates and people with doctorates. They are young, middle-aged, and retired. They live in cities, suburbs, and rural America. They have white-collar, blue-collar, pink-collar, and no-collar jobs. They have kids at home and are empty nesters. They are our neighbors. They are all around us.

They can even be us.

Tightropers and Race

In the past decades, the financial challenges facing Black Americans have become painfully clear. The poverty rate for Blacks is twice as high as the rate for whites[22] and the average Black household has 10% of the wealth of the average white household ($16,300 vs. $163,000).[23] While real income increased for Blacks during the 1990s, it has only just gotten back to the levels before the Great Recession and has remained consistently lower than white households by approximately $30,000.[24]

Is the increase in financial instability that has fueled the growth of Tightropers in this country primarily a racial issue?

The fact that there are more than 100 million Tightropers in this country—more than three times the total number of Black Americans—suggests that the issue is not purely driven by racial inequality. But are Black Tightropers fundamentally different? Do they require unique policies and services to improve their financial situation?

The Center for the New Middle Class looked into the ways that Tightropers perceive and manage their financial situations and found that Tightropers of all races and ethnicities shared significant financial stress. Remarkably, Black Tightropers were actually more confident and felt more in control of their finances than Tightropers as a whole.

CHART 1.3. Perceptions of Financial Control[25]

- ■ Black Tightropers   □ All Tightropers

The biggest difference they found between Black Tightropers and other Tightropers was how they manage debt. Blacks are far more likely to use nonbank financial products (such as payday loans) suggesting that the "de-banking" of Tightropers has hit Black households hardest.

Without a doubt, Black Americans face crippling financial challenges that need to be addressed. Over 20% live in poverty and 25% have zero or negative net worth.[26] Bob Johnson, the founder of BET, who I have worked with and have tremendous respect for, has called for $14 trillion in reparations to address structural differences and the history of racial injustice.

We must be attuned to racial differences when attempting to address the needs of Tightropers. In particular, we need to pay special attention to ensure that programs, policies, and products reach Black families. However, the macroeconomic and socioeconomic factors that have created more than 100 million Tightropers in this country impact all races and ethnicities. When we lift the prospects of all people facing financial instability, we will make an outsized difference in communities of color.

CHART 1.4. Use of Debt[27]

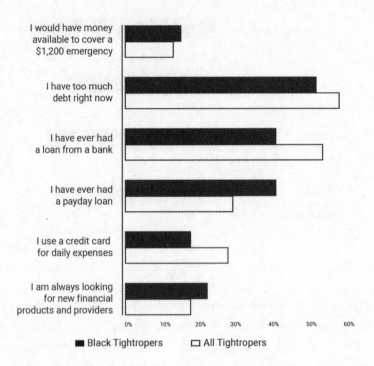

Black Tightropers   All Tightropers

Why Teetering?

Unfortunately, the typical narratives and policy recommendations from both ends of the political spectrum fail to recognize Tightropers' daily realities. The largely paternalistic policy recommendations of the political left have led to fewer financial options and pushed Tightropers out of the traditional banking system. However, unfettered deregulation from the political right has failed to deliver much-needed consumer protections for some of our most at-risk Americans.

This book is an attempt to chart a new path forward based on original research from the Center for the New Middle Class into the growth of Tightropers and their unique financial pressures and needs. This book will also introduce you to many remarkable Tightropers and connect you with the humans behind the data. You will see how they have learned to get by in a world with greater financial instability than ever before.

I believe that only through a deep understanding of and empathy for Tightropers is it possible to develop policy and product solutions that won't have unexpected and counterproductive consequences. Based on my experience serving Tightropers for nearly two decades, combined with extensive original research, this book will present a series of recommendations for both public policy changes and private sector innovation to support Tightropers, provide better safety nets, and help them find their path to financial stability.

Tackling all this will require a unified commitment from policymakers and regulators, financial institutions and Fintech disrupters, as well as Tightropers themselves. The problem is too big for any one company, government agency, or nonprofit to solve alone.

The good news for the financial services industry is that what's good for Tightropers can be good for investors and shareholders, too. I believe that so much that I started a company with the sole purpose of using new data sources and analytics to make financial services more affordable and beneficial for Tightropers.

The good news for consumer advocates, academics, and policymakers is that there are plenty of "common ground" approaches that will lead to better outcomes for American Tightropers. Some will require regulatory change and others new legislation, but we can achieve bipartisan support for solutions that will make a difference in the lives of millions.

The more Tightropers I meet, the more faith I have in them. Here's the thing about Tightropers: they usually stay on the rope! And when they fall off, they usually find a way to get back on.

They're the people I bet on every day.

When you meet them, you'll see what I mean. You'll bet on them, too.

Doing the Math: How Many Americans Are on the Financial Tightrope?

The short answer? More than 105 million. 42% of American adults.

Here is how I derived that eye-popping number (assuming 254 million American adults):[28] I start with credit scores, since they are a well-used and empirically derived indicator of financial stability. Furthermore, access to credit provides an important financial safety net for people without savings or access to family resources, and lack of credit can be destabilizing. Today, people with a credit score of 700 or greater are considered to have sufficient resources and stability to be able to repay any debt obligations with very low risk of default. However, those with less than 700 are considered "subprime" and are typically declined for traditional bank credit products.

According to FICO, the maker of the most recognized credit score, 43% of "scorable" American adults have FICO credit scores of less than 700.[29] But the Consumer Financial Protection Bureau identified an additional fifty-three million American adults—19% of the country—who are "credit invisible" or have such thin or outdated credit histories that it is impossible for the credit bureaus to estimate their creditworthiness.[30] The combination of "subprime" plus "credit invisible" plus "unscorable" represent 54% of American adults who are either currently struggling financially or are likely to struggle if they experience unexpected expenses or reductions in income.

However, the Tightropers I am writing about in this book are not destitute or without financial resources. They may struggle with limited savings and income instability, but most of the time they earn enough to pay their bills. To avoid confusion, I removed the 12% of Americans who live below the poverty line[31] and categorized them as "Down and Out" because they face far more intractable financial problems than Tightropers.

Similarly, I removed "Millionaires" from the ranks of the Safely Stable since their resources protect them from almost any realistic financial hurdles. Those with at least one million dollars in net wealth excluding the value of their residence—represent about 9% of US households.[32] Unlike Millionaires, the merely Safely Stable have adequate savings and resources to deal with most financial challenges, but could easily become Tightropers given more serious setbacks such as a deep recession, long-term job loss, or significant health issues.

2

HOW TIGHTROPERS MANAGE
LIFE'S UPS AND DOWNS

It's not savings—it's credit

- Job loss and medical expenses are what push most people off the tightrope.
- Credit is essential for Tightropers, but their needs are not the same as the Safely Stable.
- Banks are no longer the primary provider of credit to struggling Americans who have been driven to problematic but surprisingly well-liked products like payday loans, title loans, and pawn loans.

t's time to hear from our first Tightroper.[1] James is a Millennial living in California, pursuing the entrepreneurial dream. Despite his ambition and commitment, however, the reality is that most start-ups fail. And that creates tremendous financial pressure on people like James.

A few years ago, there were so many challenges in my life. I had been working for tech start-ups and as they often do, one after the other, they either got bought out or went out of business. So in between each business either selling or folding, I would spend a little time out of work, and every time I did that, my own savings would be depleted. My credit took a few hits because I didn't have the luxury of savings that I could fall back on if I had an emergency.

Once I joined the company I'm with now, it was a great relief. I was able to cover my overhead without having to worry about life in general, but I wasn't able to rebuild my finances, my credit, or my savings very quickly.

Unfortunately, I found out my teeth weren't super great. I had a gigantic dental issue with a gigantic bill attached.

I didn't have any traditional options like banks or credit cards available to me. Banks want to lend to folks who don't really need money. Their decisions are very cookie-cutter—they just care about your credit score. When your credit is compromised, they don't have any way of knowing what your situation is going to be in three months. They don't know you just started a new job and you've successfully sold quite a few things that you're going to get paid on in a few months. That's not their framework for establishing creditworthiness, which is understandable.

Going to my family wasn't something I was going to do. For me, I like to keep credit and financial decisions separate from family. It's not the kind of thing I want to talk about over Thanksgiving dinner.

Even well-meaning people often have simplistic and inaccurate perceptions of Tightropers. Over the years, I have heard a remarkable number of naïve or pejorative statements and questions about people who struggle with financial problems.

- "Aren't you just talking about poor people?"
- "They must be uneducated and undisciplined."
- "This wouldn't be a problem if they saved money every month."
- "They are just victims of predatory products."
- "Why don't they just go to their bank or a credit union?"

In the context of these statements about Tightropers, James' story is illuminating.

He's not poor (he makes good money when he's employed). He's not dumb or uneducated (he graduated from college). He's not lazy (he has joined a series of technology start-ups). He's not irresponsible (his dental problems caused his financial setback). He's not a freeloader (he refuses to ask his family for help). He's not unaware of his financial options (he has a deep understanding of how banks make credit decisions), but his real-world options are extremely limited (nonbank lenders are his only resource for credit).

James is clearly an ambitious person who is willing to work hard to get ahead—even while acknowledging the risk that things may not turn out perfectly. He takes full accountability for his life decisions and is extremely clear-eyed about the factors that led him to his current situation. He also takes pride in being able to manage whatever issues come his way without turning to family or friends for a handout. What is most remarkable about James, and so many of the Tightropers you will meet, is his deep well of optimism. He has confidence in his capabilities and is determined to ultimately succeed.

Tightropers like James don't want charity. They live rich lives balancing family, community, and, in many cases, multiple jobs. They may need support when they fall off the financial tightrope they walk every day, but that support needs to fit within their fast-paced lifestyles.

Much has been written lately about the rise in income inequality. According to a study published in the *Quarterly Journal of Economics*, we now have the largest discrepancy between the top 0.1% and the rest of the country since the Gilded Age.[2]

The rise of Tightropers, however, is not simply a matter of income inequality. In fact, Tightropers exist in almost all income bands (with the exception of the 1%).

Earlier I highlighted the fact that three-quarters of working Americans feel that they live "paycheck to paycheck" either some or all of the time. What I didn't mention is that 28% of people earning $50,000 to $99,000 feel that way along with nearly one in ten of those earning over $100,000![3]

Those living in high-cost cities like New York and San Francisco are especially vulnerable to financial fragility—even with high incomes. As we saw with James, a well-paying job at a technology start-up is less secure than an established company, and if you lose it you're still stuck with high rent and living expenses.

The financial devastation of the COVID-19 pandemic has made the instability facing Tightropers all too visible to the entire country. As restaurants, museums, conventions, sporting events, and a wide variety of gatherings shut down, the public saw how economic upheavals outside of our control can quickly disrupt commerce and income streams.

What Pushes People Off the Tightrope?

Tightropers are largely defined by their low savings rates and financial fragility. But what pushes them off the tightrope? What are the biggest drivers of financial hardship for Tightropers?

For James, it was a toxic mixture of job loss and an unexpected medical expense. He is not unique in this. The top drivers of financial stress for Americans are job loss and medical bills.

Of course, all of us deal with financial setbacks on occasion. Even people with significant resources are impacted by drops in the stock market, job changes, or large unexpected expenses. However, Tightropers are different because financial setbacks for them can have life-changing impacts.

To better understand the unique drivers of financial stress in the lives of Tightropers, the Center for the New Middle Class asked people with low credit scores to list the specific events in their lives that caused their credit score to drop below 700. People with credit scores below 700 are considered subprime and are typically declined for credit by traditional banks. A financial event that causes such a dramatic reduction in a credit score can fairly be considered life-changing.

The top reasons for significant credit erosion are job loss and medical bills, with car repair coming behind (along with a variety of other discrete events like moving to a new home or helping a child pay for college).

Life emergencies are financial emergencies. And life happens…a lot.

According to research by Bankrate,[4] in approximately two-thirds of situations where Americans experienced what they termed a "significant unexpected expense," the expense was less than $5,000. But even this can be financially devastating. The Center for the New Middle Class found that Tightropers can only weather an unexpected expense equivalent to 31% of their monthly income. For Tightropers living paycheck to paycheck with limited savings, an unexpected bill can become a crisis when it exceeds $1,400.[5]

CHART 2.1. Causes of Financial Stress[6]

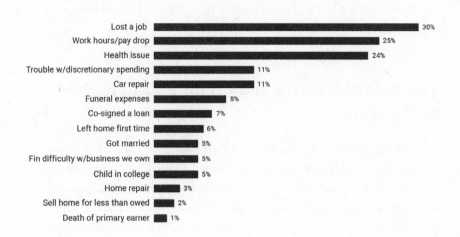

Lost a job	30%
Work hours/pay drop	25%
Health issue	24%
Trouble w/discretionary spending	11%
Car repair	11%
Funeral expenses	8%
Co-signed a loan	7%
Left home first time	6%
Got married	5%
Fin difficulty w/business we own	5%
Child in college	5%
Home repair	3%
Sell home for less than owed	2%
Death of primary earner	1%

Long-term medical problems (either for Tightropers or their family members) can be far more catastrophic, and in many cases can't realistically be managed through short-term financial support. What's unique and particularly pernicious about medical expenses is that they are often combined with job loss or reduction in pay. In fact, of those who identified medical bills as a primary cause of credit erosion, three-quarters also experienced an income drop, severely complicating their ability to manage and cover medical expenses.

Tellingly, according to GoFundMe's CEO, one-third of donations on that website go to pay for medical expenses in one form or another.[7] The COVID-19 pandemic is a particularly extreme example of the healthcare pitfalls Tightropers have historically faced.

One other remarkable takeaway from the Center for the New Middle Class study is that many of the causes of financial upheaval in the lives of Tightropers aren't even due to their own setbacks. As will be reinforced in many of the stories you will hear from Tightropers, many of their financial struggles stem from their commitment and compassion for helping others.

While Tightropers are often uncomfortable asking family and friends for financial support, they may be called upon to provide it to others. Whether it is helping children with their college education or getting their first apartment, supporting parents or other family members with declining health, or being there to help friends with financial challenges,

Tightropers take these responsibilities seriously. In many ways, their reluctance to ask friends and family for financial support stems from an acute awareness of the hardship this can bring.

The Role of Savings and Credit as Safety Nets for Tightropers

It should go without saying that reduced savings is a central factor in the rapid growth of Tightropers in this country. Due to declining savings rates and the wealth-eroding impact of increasing income instability—not to mention the lingering impacts of the Great Recession and the COVID-19 pandemic—the "nest egg" that we all strive for doesn't exist for Tightropers. If faced with even a minor financial emergency, most Tightropers would not have enough money on hand to pay out of pocket.

According to a study by the Center for the New Middle Class, 70% of Tightropers couldn't cover an urgent $500 expense with their savings. Furthermore, only 36% felt that they could borrow $500 from a family member or friend. For a $2,000 financial need, the number dropped to barely 20%.[8]

Without savings or family and friends with deep pockets, how do Tightropers manage through financial setbacks? Credit.

Access to credit is an essential safety net for Tightropers and supports them through financial ups and downs the way savings supports the Safely Stable. While there are problems with many of the nonbank credit products widely available to Tightropers, for struggling Americans, the highest-cost form of credit is often no credit at all.

Without a cash cushion of savings or access to credit, Tightropers can face terrible consequences from a financial setback. They might be able to absorb one financial hit—say, to replace a refrigerator for $1,500—but if that wipes out their limited savings, they won't be able to cover their daughter's visit to the emergency room when she breaks her arm playing soccer. And if they can't afford to repair their car, they could lose their job.

A number of years back, the general counsel of my company was speaking with an attorney general in a state that aggressively opposed any sort of higher-interest credit products. As a result of this stance, access to credit was extremely limited and only people with very high credit scores were able to borrow to cover unexpected expenses. When she asked him what he thought people should do if they couldn't get a loan, he said in his state they could use "the Boot."

My general counsel hadn't heard of this "Boot" before and thought it might have been a nickname for some sort of social welfare program, so she asked about it. He said that in his state, if you needed some extra money, you held out a boot at the side of the road and people would put money in it.

His solution to the need for credit was panhandling!

Back in the real world, it should be clear that access to at least limited amounts of credit is an important safety net for Tightropers and is far better than forcing people to beg for money on street corners or sell their possessions under duress. However, the way Tightropers select and use credit is very different from those with more financial resources and less financial stress.

When Tightropers need credit, it is typically urgent. Unlike prime consumers, they don't have time to stand in line at a bank, fill out lots of paperwork, and wait days to be approved and funded. They need a quick decision with no hassles and cash in their account as soon as possible. Remember, access to cash could be the thing that stands in the way of repairing their car or getting medical care for their child.

As a result, Tightropers overwhelmingly list attributes such as speed and ease of the application process as critical to them when selecting a credit provider—assuming they can get enough credit to solve their financial need. Transparency and credit-building are also important to Tightropers. However, barely 15% of Tightropers list "lowest APR" in their top three objectives for credit.

Given the urgency of financial need, Tightropers are unsurprisingly much more focused on a speedy and hassle-free application process than the Safely Stable. However, Tightropers are well-aware of their damaged credit scores and ongoing financial vulnerability, and as a result are also more interested in credit building, reasonable collection practices, and payment flexibility in case they become unable to repay the loan.

CHART 2.2. Most Important Criteria for Credit[9]

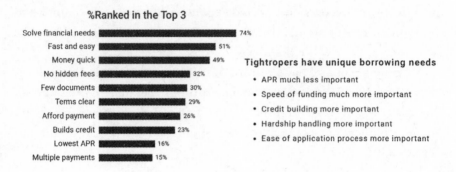

%Ranked in the Top 3

Solve financial needs	74%
Fast and easy	51%
Money quick	49%
No hidden fees	32%
Few documents	30%
Terms clear	29%
Afford payment	26%
Builds credit	23%
Lowest APR	16%
Multiple payments	15%

Tightropers have unique borrowing needs

- APR much less important
- Speed of funding much more important
- Credit building more important
- Hardship handling more important
- Ease of application process more important

FICO Scores—The New Scarlet Letter

Back before my time—a hundred years ago—bankers would make loans based on personal character. The image of the friendly small-town banker who would grant you a loan based on your personal character was immortalized by George Bailey, the hero of the classic movie *It's a Wonderful Life.* Today, algorithms and formulas try to crystallize character into a single number: the credit score, typically the well-known FICO score pioneered by Bill Fair and Earl Isaac in the 1950s.

A FICO score is the industry term for the credit score which assigns every "scorable" person a rating from 300 to 850. More than 20% of Americans don't have a FICO score at all, and about 16% are in the 300–599 range, considered "very poor." Another 18% are in the 600–699 range, considered "poor" to "fair." People with low FICO scores—along with credit invisibles—are typically declined for credit by banks. This is largely because FICO is a pretty good indicator of risk, and people with low FICO scores generally have a high risk of default. Note, however, that a credit score is a risk summary. It says nothing about someone's available cash, net worth, income, or job prospects.

Credit scores have become so fundamental in our lives that they can have a greater impact than almost any other rating—more important than grades, SAT scores, or number of Twitter followers. Not only do they impact the availability and cost of credit, they are also used by human resources departments to determine whether to offer employment and by rental agencies to determine whether to approve housing. Credit scores are also used to determine how much of a down payment is required to rent a house and whether a cell phone customer needs to pay in advance for services.

CHART 2.3. Distribution of FICO Scores[10]

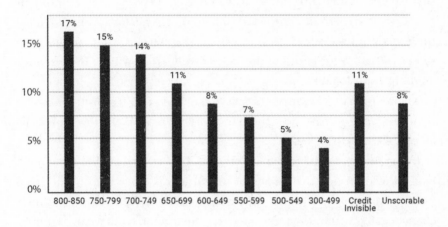

It is the Scarlet Letter of our time. If you have a low credit score, you are shunned by businesses. According to a study by the Center for the New Middle Class, it may also impact dating. They found that female Tightropers are more likely to say they've had a relationship unravel because of their partner's finances and more likely to say they've had a partner who was dishonest about finances.[11] It's not hard to imagine that soon dating apps will use credit scores to determine who gets "swiped left."

It isn't easy to build or repair damaged credit scores, nor is it obvious how to do it. A wide variety of credit-related data is used to determine credit scores, including previous use of credit, utilization rates of existing credit facilities, and derogatory information such as late payments, charge-offs, and bankruptcies. Use of credit is a good thing, but too much use is a bad thing. These criteria are continually being updated and, as a result, it's hard for people to determine the best and fastest way to rebuild their credit scores.

Unfortunately, credit scores are particularly inaccurate when it comes to people with low credit scores. As Leo Tolstoy wrote in *Anna Karenina*,

"All happy families are alike; each unhappy family is unhappy in its own way." Likewise, people with good credit are alike. They have lots of experience with credit and very little negative history.

For Tightropers, the situation is different. They may have no credit history at all because they don't trust banks. Or they may have had an expensive divorce and declared bankruptcy years ago but now have a well-paying, stable job and savings. Or they may just be temporarily over-extended on their credit cards due to recent job loss. Although all of these people have very different financial situations, their poor credit scores will almost guarantee the same result—they will be declined for credit by traditional banks.

The real story of Tightropers isn't told in their credit scores. It's told in their resilience, persistence, and hard work as they use the few tools available to them to bridge cash gaps.

In the future, access to expanded data sources may enable a new generation of underwriting tools that will function more like the fictional George Bailey to see the true financial situation of Tightropers and their character, ability, and willingness to repay their debt. Until then, Tightropers will continue to be unfairly stigmatized by credit scores.

Why Banks No Longer Serve Tightropers

Deon is another Tightroper. He reminds us that financial challenges quickly turn into relationship challenges and impact many parts of our life. And without access to credit, managing through life's downturns can be difficult.

> *I ran out of gas in front of my recruiting station in high school and figured that a higher power was calling me to serve my country. I was in the Navy and saw the world and learned a lot. Now I'm in sales. And as anyone in sales knows, income fluctuates. You have your good months and your bad months. I should know, I've been at it for over a decade.*
>
> *I also have a side business with my wife, but our business partner left us hanging and it created a real burden on us. We had budgeted carefully but all of a sudden we were stuck with bills—it was really tough for my wife emotionally.*

I'd taken payday loans in the past, but they can get you caught in a cycle. It's a small amount, but then you go every couple of weeks and renew the loan and before long there's no end in sight. And even with all the payments it's not like your credit score gets any better.

And it's not like I can get money from a bank. You've got to have a decent credit history and they ask you to provide bank statements and your blood type and everything else. And you still don't get anything!

Tightropers vary in a lot of important ways, but one trait seems to come through again and again—they don't like or trust banks. They feel they aren't wanted and aren't adequately served, and as a result they aren't comfortable with old-school banks.

Unlike people with good credit, only about one-third of Tightropers feel that their bank would approve them for a credit card or personal loan. In fact, only a quarter of Tightropers think their bank even has credit products that fit their needs.[12] Remember, Tightropers need access to relatively small amounts of credit but they need it quickly and with minimal hassle. This is not the way banks typically work. No surprise that Tightropers don't feel banks are focused on their needs!

CHART 2.4. Perspectives on Banks[13]

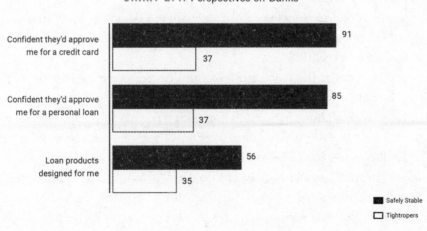

Credit cards, the mainstay of consumer credit in the US, don't work well for Tightropers. If Tightropers are approved for a credit card at all, it typically has very low availability (that is, the amount customers can borrow) of just a few hundred dollars and high annual fees. In some cases, credit card companies may require the consumer to pledge cash deposits against the card, which can be challenging for cash-strapped Tightropers.

Tightropers instead may be forced to use bank overdraft protection programs strategically, to cover expenses when they don't have sufficient cash. This might seem like a smart move until you realize the actual cost of these programs. According to the Federal Deposit Insurance Corporation (FDIC), overdraft protection charges have an effective APR of over 3,500%![14]

It's not just credit products. Tightropers have become frustrated with banks for a wide variety of reasons. Tightropers typically don't get bank services for free, unlike their better-credit neighbors, and are nearly three times more likely to pay fees to their financial institutions.[15]

The de-banking of Tightropers has been happening for decades but accelerated after the Great Recession. Based on a simplistic and inaccurate belief that subprime lending caused the financial crisis, regulators pressured banks to tighten credit standards dramatically,[16] resulting in an estimated $143 billion reduction in subprime consumer credit in the US.[17] This dramatically shrunk the financial safety net for American Tightropers and helped fuel the growth of higher interest nonbank financial products like payday loans and title loans.

There is reason to believe this can change. Regulators seem to be increasingly aware that they may have gone too far in pushing banks to restrict access to credit.

Joseph Otting, the Comptroller of the Currency, wrote in 2018 that "banks, right or wrong, have exited [subprime lending] and there appears to be a large vacuum. We would encourage people to present business models to us for our review [detailing] how they would like to serve it."[18]

Furthermore, banks are starting to understand the problem as well. A president of a large regional bank told me privately that "the average FICO score of customers I provide credit to is 720–740, but the average FICO score of customers opening up checking accounts is 560–580—I literally don't have any credit products for them." In order to grow and better serve their core customers, banks are going to have to figure out how to start saying "yes" again to the Tightropers that they've ignored for so long.

Payday, Pawn, and Title—Sharks or Saviors?

As we have discussed, banks no longer effectively serve the day-to-day consumer credit needs of Tightropers. In the past, banks were seen as the primary financial institution for the average American. Now, because of regulatory pressures, cumbersome and slow processes, and a failure to innovate new underwriting approaches that work for people with damaged credit scores, Tightropers have largely given up on their local bank branches.

Instead, Tightropers increasingly see nonbank lenders such as payday lenders, title lenders, pawn and storefront and online installment lenders as their primary source of short-term credit. This is what has driven the astonishing growth of the industry over the past few decades, resulting in more payday loan stores than McDonald's in the US.[19]

Innumerable articles have been written about payday lenders and other nonbank, subprime-oriented lenders. We are told that they are too high cost, that they can lead to a cycle of debt, and that they are predatory.

What we aren't told is that customers generally like them.

Customer satisfaction scores for these credit products are typically higher than most banks. A survey of payday loan customers found that the majority of borrowers said they were happy with the product and 65% stated that they were likely or very likely to recommend payday loans to family or friends. A remarkable 98% said they were satisfied with their experience.[20]

This is because these products fit very well with the needs of Tightropers. They are easy to apply for, fast to get, and simple to understand. Simply vilifying them without providing better credit alternatives for underserved Americans is short-sighted and may actually harm Tightropers. One study by the New York Federal Reserve Bank reported that when payday loans are banned it leads to an increase in bank overdraft fees and bankruptcies.[21]

Furthermore, payday lenders are highly regulated and, even in their current flawed form, are not at the top of Tightropers' worries. In late 2018, the Consumer Financial Protection Bureau reported that complaints against payday lenders were not in the top five problematic categories (credit reports and debt collection drew, by far, the most complaints) and were declining (actually less than 2% of overall complaints).[22]

Every month, millions of Americans take out short-term, high-interest loans. They turn to short-term loans because they urgently need money for unexpected emergencies, or to bridge a cash shortage for their businesses, or because just one piece of their financial puzzle didn't fit that month.

When they go to a payday lender—in a storefront location or online—they know what they are getting into. And they get into it because they have few other options. Furthermore, unlike bank branches that don't want their business, nonbank lenders are excited to serve them and are friendly, welcoming, and nonjudgmental.

That having been said, payday loans, title loans, and pawn loans are all deeply flawed products. Let's look at them individually:

Payday loans are essentially a two-week loan meant to bridge a customer until their next paycheck. The customer writes a post-dated check or gives the lender access to debit their bank account (typically customers need to have a checking account), and on their next payday they repay the advance with a fee—anywhere from 15% to 25% on average. This has an effective annual percentage rate (APR) that can range from 350% to over 600%.

A payday loan is one of the easiest credit products to understand and has no hidden fees. Consumers can easily determine the cost and decide whether they can afford it and how it compares to other alternatives. The problem, however, is that Tightropers are rarely able to recover from a financial setback that quickly. They typically don't have the money in two weeks to fully repay the debt, so they just take out another loan by paying the fee and "rolling over" the principal. This is the troublesome "cycle of debt" that consumer advocates rail against, and they have a point.

Title loans can be even more financially destructive. Unlike a payday loan, which is unsecured, title loans require customers to pledge their cars as collateral. Although title loans are usually less expensive than payday loans ("only" 300% effective APR),[23] if the customer can't repay it in time, they can lose their car. And according to the Consumer Financial Protection Agency, over 20% of all title loan customers will ultimately lose their car to the title lender.[24] This is particularly troubling since, as we discussed earlier, one of the biggest drivers of financial stress for Tightropers is car repair and maintaining the ongoing ability to drive to work.

Pawn lending is often referred to as the second-oldest profession. As such, it rarely receives the focus and vitriol from consumers, groups, and regulators that goes to payday and title loans. However, it's just as problematic as the other products for serving the needs of Tightropers.

With a pawn loan, customers bring in a personal good (a watch, a wedding ring, etc.) and leave it as collateral for a loan that is much less than the value of the pawned item. Not only is this inconvenient and embarrassing, if they are unable to repay the loan and lose the collateral, the effective APR can be far higher than either of the above products.

We Can—and Must—Do Better for Tightropers

Tightropers like the ones we've heard from—James and Deon—are the new mainstream in this country. They are hardworking and understand their real-world options. They don't always make optimal financial decisions—who does!—but they want to be responsible and even go the extra mile to help their loved ones. However, without improved financial safety nets, their lives can quickly fall prey to even relatively minor financial setbacks.

Simply banning nonbank credit products or instituting rate caps that make them unprofitable may seem appealing, but as we've shown, access to credit is a vital safety net for Tightropers facing financial stress. Without them, Tightropers will find it hard to pay their bills and be able to take their children to the doctor or their pets to the vet. Asking them to simply use "the Boot" to beg for help isn't helpful either.

Tightropers deserve better than these products. They deserve products and policies that can help them build savings. They deserve access to credit that is fast and flexible enough to meet their financial needs yet comes with far less potential financial harm than these "legacy" products.

3

THE POLITICS OF TIGHTROPERS

Tightropers are a distinct and frustrated voting bloc

- Tightropers are less vocal but have political interests that are different than the Safely Stable.
- Socially, they care most about childcare, elder assistance, and protecting welfare.
- Fiscally, they are concerned about income inequality, social security reform, and college education costs.
- Attitudinally, they have confidence in their personal abilities to manage through life's changes, but are more pessimistic than the Safely Stable.

"We in America do not have government by the majority. We have government by the majority who participate."   —*attributed to Thomas Jefferson.*[1]

Politicians should care about Tightropers simply because they make up almost half the country and are struggling financially right now. However, politicians should also care because Tightropers may determine the outcome of elections and they're not happy with the status quo.

As a Tightroper named Linda harshly declared about our political system: "They just don't get it. The far left is only worried about the poor—which I'm not—and the far right isn't even trying to help."

Linda is not alone in being frustrated with the major political parties. Tightropers are 50% more likely than the Safely Stable to have no strong party affiliation. This may explain why so many people who voted for Obama switched to Trump—they look for the person (not the party) who best speaks to their issues.

CHART 3.1. Party Affiliation—Tightroper vs Safely Stable[2]

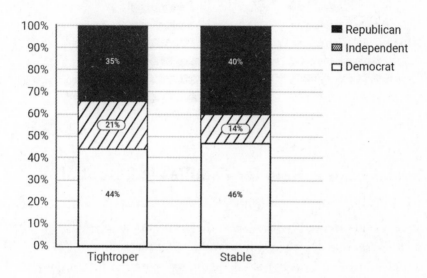

One of the challenges for understanding the perspectives of Tightropers is that, other than online posting, Tightropers are much less engaged in any sort of political discourse than the Safely Stable, so their voice is not as loud. It will be critical for both political parties to listen closely to the concerns of all Americans—including the silent majority of Tightropers—not just the more vocal Safely Stable.

This has tremendous implications for political parties. The candidates who reach out, deeply understand, and passionately articulate the concerns of Tightropers will likely win elections for years to come.

To better understand the unique political concerns and attitudes of Tightropers, the Center for The New Middle Class asked Tightropers and the Safely Stable to rank the importance of a sweeping number of social and fiscal concerns. The differences strike to the heart of the Tightroper experience and unique stresses.

CHART 3.2. Political Participation—Tightroper vs Safely Stable

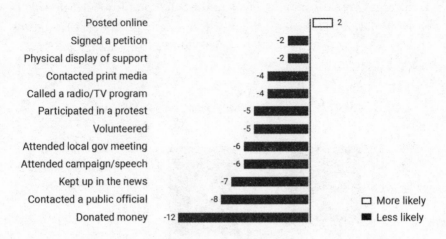

Posted online	2
Signed a petition	-2
Physical display of support	-2
Contacted print media	-4
Called a radio/TV program	-4
Participated in a protest	-5
Volunteered	-5
Attended local gov meeting	-6
Attended campaign/speech	-6
Kept up in the news	-7
Contacted a public official	-8
Donated money	-12

☐ More likely
■ Less likely

Social Issues: Help for Families is Essential

The Center for the New Middle Class asked respondents to rank eigh-teen "social-oriented" issues based on "importance to you." The issues that emerged as "extremely important" (the top rating out of five) by both Tightropers and the Safely Stable were driven by contemporary news coverage:

1. Personal data security (50%)[3]
2. Terrorism prevention (48%)
3. Racial equality (40%)
4. Gun control/rights (39%)
5. Environment protection (38%)

Many issues discussed by political pundits didn't make the cut. In par-ticular, election reform, union/worker rights, humanitarian rights, and regulatory reform were only of passing interest to both Tightropers and the Safely Stable. Although unions were historically a critical concern for the working class of the past, they are no longer broadly seen as a relevant issue for the current generation of workers.

However, Tightropers and the Safely Stable diverged on certain social-oriented issues. Tightropers were far more concerned about childcare, elder assistance, and protecting welfare. The first two should come as no surprise, since childcare and elder assistance are such huge financial and psychological drains on Tightroper families. The fact that welfare is a big concern suggests that Tightropers—although in many ways optimistic about their futures—want to make sure they have a safety net if things don't work out. It also suggests that they may have more hard-earned empathy for those even less fortunate than they are.

CHART 3.3. Relative Importance of Social Issues

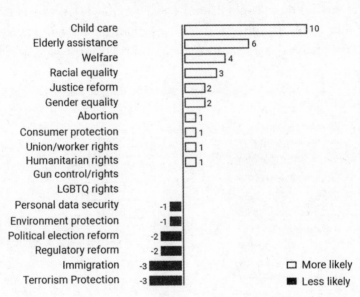

Fiscal Policy Issues: Healthcare is a Killer

The overall ranking of concerns about fiscal policy-related issues should also come as no surprise.

1. Healthcare (54%)
2. Retirement Support (38%)

3.   Social Security (38%)
4.   Income Inequality (38%)
5.   Energy Costs (36%)[4]

With regard to fiscal policy issues, the pundits on the political right seem to have it wrong. Perennial Republican topics such as tax reform, corporate tax rates, trade agreements, and tariffs all ranked at the bottom of the respondents' concerns. Either they don't matter to the average American, or Republicans have done a poor job of explaining why they should.

Similar to social issues, what is particularly striking is how much Tight-ropers vary on these issues from the Safely Stable. Tightropers focus on economic issues that directly drive their financial well-being, such as income inequality, social security reform, and college education costs.

CHART 3.4. Relative Importance of Fiscal Issues

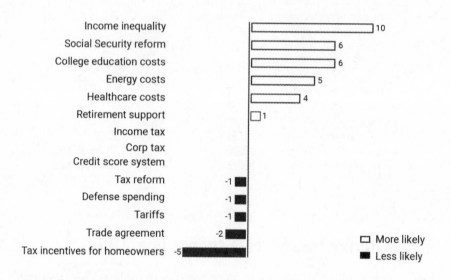

Attitudinal Issues—
Confident in Themselves, Not the Government

The study also asked respondents to state how much they agreed or dis-agreed with a series of "attitudinal statements." The statements related to confidence in their personal ability to succeed financially, the political system, and whether political parties understand and support their needs.

Despite the frustrations and genuine challenges facing so many Americans today, both Tightropers and the Safely Stable largely demonstrate confidence in their ability to manage their financial lives. Between 60% and 70% of both Tightropers and the Safely Stable agreed with statements like "I know how to improve my financial stability" and "I'm optimistic about my future." This should be tremendously reassuring to those who care about the future of the country. We are still a country of scrappy achievers who believe in our innate ability to get ahead.

Americans have considerably less confidence in their government and elected representatives. That should be a wake-up call to both political parties. In almost all cases, respondents ranked statements about their ability to manage their lives higher than that of the government and political parties to help them.

Some of the lowest attitudinal responses were for statements like the following:

- I trust the federal government to make good decisions for the country (33%)
- Elected officials care about people like me (32%)
- Government works for people like me (31%)
- I feel like my voice is heard in the political system (27%)
- I believe the government spends tax dollars wisely (25%)

The health of our democracy is at stake when over two-thirds of Americans do not feel that the government has their best interest at heart. This sentiment is driving the rise of openly socialist politicians on the left and openly nativist politicians on the right. Both are symptoms of the fact that people do not feel that things are "right" or fair for people like them.

This is particularly true of Tightropers who are far more pessimistic across all of the attitudinal questions than the Safely Stable.

CHART 3.5. Relative Importance of Attitudinal Issues

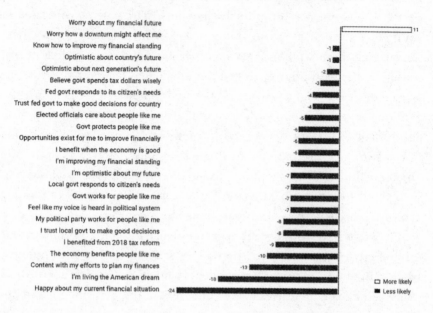

No wonder Tightropers are less involved in the political system than the Safely Stable. Leaders need to rethink their talking points and policy perspectives to reengage this underrepresented but hardworking and caring group of Americans. Those in power—whether the media, politicians, or industry leaders—need to start reaching out and listening to Tightropers.

How to Read the Charts in this Chapter

The Center for the New Middle Class surveyed Tightropers and the Safely Stable to better understand their unique concerns and political differences. The charts in this chapter highlight the differences between the groups but can be confusing to read.

The numbers on the charts are not absolute values, but rather the differences between the responses given by Tightropers and the Safely Stable. For instance, 33% of the Safely Stable responded that they donated money to political candidates, while only 21% of the Tightropers gave the same answer. As a result, the chart will show -12, which is the difference in percentage points between Tightropers and the Safely Stable. I've adopted this methodology to easily indicate the biggest points of divergence between the groups.

4

TIGHTROPERS IN THE AGE OF COVID-19

We're all a pandemic away from being Tightropers

- The COVID-19 pandemic accelerated awareness of income instability across the entire economy almost overnight.
- Tightropers are accustomed to these financial pressures and adapted better than the Safely Stable.
- Governmental policies to address pandemic-related financial stress were largely wasted on unsustainable giveaways.
- COVID-19 should be a call to action to create improved policies and services for current Tightropers as well as those that future pandemics may create.

One of the great myths of this country is that we can control our destiny by working hard, sacrificing, and making the "right" decisions in our lives. Best-selling financial self-help books reinforce this view. Dave Ramsay provides "a proven plan for financial success," Tony Robbins offers "7 simple steps to financial freedom," and no less an authority than 50 Cent tells us that we just need to "hustle harder, hustle faster" to be successful.

Rationally, most of us realize that this isn't really true. We are aware of the macroeconomic trends that make it increasingly difficult to fully control our financial destiny. However, until recently, this still seemed like a problem for other people, not ourselves.

COVID upended our sense of security and control overnight. Jonathan Walker, the head of the Center for the New Middle Class, said, "the COVID-19 pandemic laid bare the lie that by being responsible you can avoid financial struggles." One unexpected implication of this horrific healthcare and financial crisis, according to Jonathan, is that it has "democratized the economic struggles" faced every day by Tightropers in America. Whereas pre-COVID, we could attribute the erosion in savings and wealth experienced by more than 100 million Tightropers as the result of bad decisions, now we are all painfully aware of how things outside of our control can make the best-laid plans go awry.

A Twin Health and Economic Crisis

By the end of 2020, COVID-19 cases in the country topped 10 million, leading to more than 250,000 deaths.[1] For context, less than 60,000 Americans were killed in the Vietnam War and less than 120,000 in World War I (World War II resulted in over 400,000 US deaths).

The death rate is staggering, as is the impact on the economy.

In the first 16 weeks following the federal declaration of a state of emergency, more than 50 million American workers filed unemployment claims.[2] The COVID-19 Eviction Defense Project in Denver estimated that as many as 20% of renters—19–23 million Americans—would be at risk of eviction due to the crisis.[3]

To understand the evolving financial impact of the COVID-19 pandemic on Americans, the Center for the New Middle Class began a series of in-depth surveys of Tightropers and the Safely Stable almost immediately after it was identified in March. Unsurprisingly, they found that concern about job loss was far greater for Tightropers. Perceptions of employment stability by Tightropers quickly dropped from above 80% to barely 70% while the Safely Stable only saw a 2% reduction in confidence about job stability. These concerns are valid since job loss has been far from uniform. According to a detailed study of Labor Department data by the *Wall Street Journal* completed in July 2020,[4] well-educated, more established, and older employees were the least impacted by pandemic-related unemployment and recovered the fastest. As of June 2020, people aged 16–24 still had employment rates 20% lower than before the pandemic and those without a college degree were facing 25% higher levels of unemployment. This contrasted with older workers with at least a bachelor's degree who faced less initial unemployment and had already recovered to nearly pre-COVID levels. This is not to suggest that the Safely Stable are immune to a broad shutdown of the US economy, but that they are less vulnerable than Tightropers.

CHART 4.1. Percentage Who Believe Their Current Employment is Stable[5]

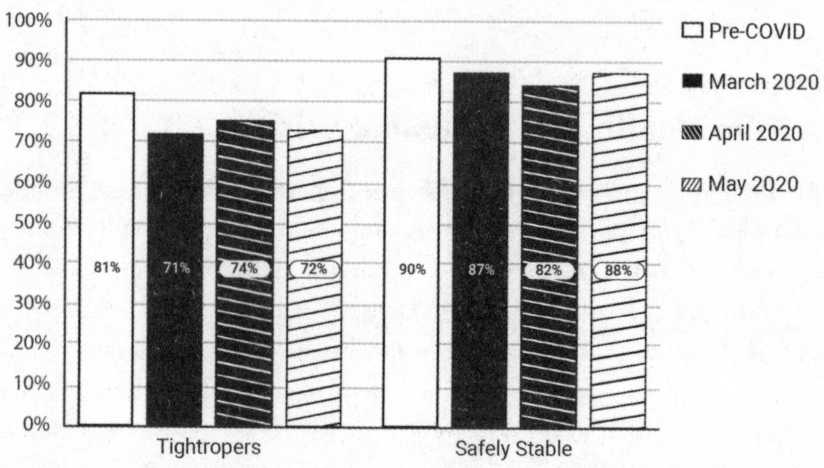

Job loss was just one aspect of the pandemic's economic devastation. Even for those who managed to retain their jobs, many experienced reduced wages due to cutbacks in hours or fewer "side hustles." Across the country, American families reported shrinking household income, according to research from the Center for the New Middle Class. For the Safely Stable, the percentage of households who experienced recent income reduction grew from 14% before COVID to 24% three months later. However, the percentage of Tightropers reporting a reduction in income grew from 28% to 37% over the same period. This means that over one-third of all Tightropers were living on less income than the previous year.

CHART 4.2. Percentage Who Experienced Reduced Household Income[6]

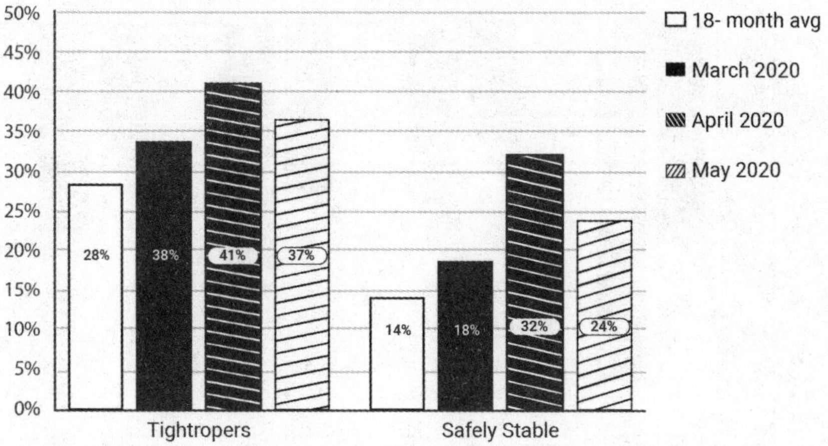

Legend:
- □ 18- month avg
- ■ March 2020
- ▨ April 2020
- ▨ May 2020

Tightropers: 28%, 38%, 41%, 37%
Safely Stable: 14%, 18%, 32%, 24%

Impact on the Credit Markets— Counter-Intuitive Results

As a result of the worst health and economic crisis to hit the US in nearly a century, the rapid erosion in the financial well-being of Tightropers comes as no surprise. Our instincts warn of credit defaults on one hand and massive increases in borrowing on the other.

The truth is exactly the opposite. The credit markets saw a dramatic drop in demand almost immediately following awareness of the pandemic. According to a study by the Consumer Financial Protection Bureau, in the first four weeks of March 2020, credit inquiries (a leading indicator of market demand) were far lower across all asset classes. Credit inquiries for auto loans dropped by over 50%; for mortgages by over 25%; and for credit cards by nearly 40%.

Nor did credit defaults for Tightropers skyrocket. The largest publicly traded nonprime lenders all reported very strong credit quality despite the loss of income among their target customers. Elevate, Curo, Enova, and One Main Financial all noted a significant reduction in originations (over 64% year over year reduction for One Main) but either flat or improved chargeoff rates! This coincided with a record increase in savings rates across the country.[7]

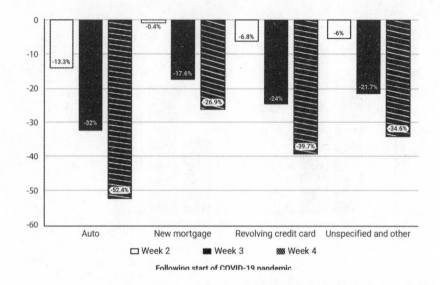

CHART 4.3. Percent Change in Credit Inquiries by Category[8]

Rather than using debt to maintain their lifestyles, Tightropers found ways to pay down their expensive credit—often with so-called "stimulus checks" from the government. According to the Center for the New Middle Class, in the months after the pandemic started in the US, Tightropers reduced their debt to the degree that 10% fewer people reported having more debt than savings.

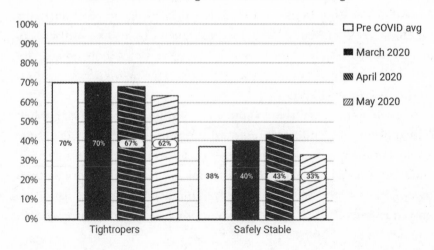

CHART 4.4. Percentage with More Debt Than Savings[9]

This demonstrates very clearly one of the most important aspects of Tightropers—they generally act responsibly with their money. Like everyone, when times are good, they assume they will continue. However, in a post-COVID world with economic uncertainty, they wisely constrained spending and used stimulus money to pay down debt—especially higher-interest debt.

The cliché about Tightropers is that they manage through tough times because they "always live in a recession." There is something to this concept. Tightropers are defined by income instability and low savings rates so they are more used to rapid adjustments in their financial lives when they face yet another setback—whether from job loss, an unexpected expense, or a global pandemic.

I think a deeper insight is that they are the "canary in the coal mine" of our society. They have learned to react rapidly to economic changes and are the first to adjust their financial situation to new realities. This response to the pandemic ultimately impacted financial providers across all credit tiers. Large "prime" lenders like Lending Club, Prosper, and SoFi all announced large layoffs due to reduced demand for debt.

Pandemic Response— Unplanned, Unfocused, and Unsustainable

Another aspect of COVID-19 that deserves analysis was the government response. As the reality set in about the near and longer-term economic impact of the pandemic, the federal government took rapid and remarkably bipartisan action to provide economic assistance to those who lost income and to stimulate economic growth. The first major legislation was the Coronavirus Aid, Relief, and Economic Security (CARES) Act, signed into law on March 27, 2020.

At a cost of over $2 trillion (and with less than two weeks of legislative effort), the CARES Act was the largest economic stimulus and relief package in history, representing 10% of gross domestic product (GDP) or *nearly half of all federal government expenditures during 2019.*[10]

Some of the main components include:

- **$1,200 Relief Checks:** Approximately 160 million checks totaling nearly $270 billion were mailed to workers making less than $75,000 a year.
- **Paycheck Protection Program (PPP) for Small Businesses:** $670 billion in loans (with an average size of more than $100,000) were funded to over 5 million companies. These loans have a 1% interest rate and are expected to be completely forgiven.
- **Main Street Lending Program (MSLP):** $600 billion in loans went to larger companies with annual revenues of up to $5 billion. These loans must be repaid but have relatively low interest rates of LIBOR plus 3%.
- **Unemployment Benefits:** $600 per week was added to regular state unemployment benefits and they were extended from 26 weeks to 39 weeks.
- **Relaxed Rules for 401(k) Loans:** Penalties for tapping into 401(k) accounts were eliminated to ease access to savings.

For the most part, these were poorly designed and implemented programs that will increase the national debt without fundamentally improving pandemic-related economic stress. Given the lack of preparedness for a global pandemic, this should come as no surprise. According to an article in the *Wall Street Journal*, the top US agency responsible for pandemic preparedness, the office for the Assistant Secretary for Preparedness and Response (ASPR), was far more focused on military threats from biological weapons than pandemics and was woefully unprepared for the impact of COVID-19 on healthcare and the economy.[11]

Sadly, much of the CARES Act brings to mind a quote often attributed to Alexis de Tocqueville: "The American Republic will endure until the day Congress discovers that it can bribe the public with the public's money."

The most popular aspect of the CARES Act was arguably the most irresponsible. A $1,200 giveaway to the majority of Americans seems like a great thing. The intent was to help Americans impacted by COVID-19 and generate economic growth.

The problem with simply handing out cash is that it doesn't go to the people who need it most and it rarely has the anticipated impact. And given the massive scale of the program, it's ultimately unaffordable.

While stimulus checks were undoubtedly a win for Tightropers and helped them improve their financial situation, they were a "shotgun" give-away rather than a laser-focused intervention for the people directly impacted by job loss due to COVID-19. As an example, my mother-in-law, who is in her 80s and lives on social security income, received a stimulus check despite not seeing any reduction in her income nor increase in her expenses. She merely deposited the check in her bank account for a time when she might need the extra money.

Nor did the checks "stimulate" the economy. The Center for the New Middle Class study indicated that one of the biggest uses of the money was for debt reduction. Smart for Tightropers, but not likely to help jumpstart a moribund economy. And this isn't even taking into account the fact that $1.4 billion in stimulus checks were mailed to dead people![12]

The Paycheck Protection Program also yielded most of its benefit to companies that didn't need it. It was such an attractive program that it was almost an IQ test for business owners. Who wouldn't want a 1% loan that you didn't have to pay back later? If you were a strong company it was free money, and if you were likely to fail (let's say you ran a struggling restaurant) you might as well take the money since there were no repercussions from defaulting on the loans.

In full disclosure, my start-up company took advantage of the program and we received over $100,000. In our situation, COVID-19 negatively impacted demand for consumer credit and we used the money for payroll during a delicate stage in the development of the company. However, 220 publicly traded companies also took loans from the program. Treasury Secretary Steve Mnuchin criticized many large corporations—including the Los Angeles Lakers who received $4.5 million—for abusing the program, saying "I think it was inappropriate for most of these companies to take loans, and we don't think they ever should have been allowed to."[13]

Another problem with the CARES Act was the relaxation of controls and penalties for 401(k) withdrawals and loans. Although the elimination of the 10% penalty for early withdrawal seems fair for people impacted by

COVID or resulting unemployment, as a society we are kicking the can on economic hardship that will only be felt once the dust settles and people face the implications of their decisions.

Pulling savings from 401(k)s will result in both long-term and short-term hardship for Tightropers. Obviously, this decimates long-term savings that will be needed for a comfortable retirement. Additionally, because of the slapdash rule-making, we can expect that people will face near-term financial hardships as they struggle with tax payments related to the withdrawals. The CFPB went so far as to urge people to be careful with 401(k) withdrawals because of tax liabilities that aren't withheld by the government. On their website they included this casually worded note of caution: "So, you may not want to spend the full amount you withdraw because you might owe some of that money in taxes later."[14]

Not all components of the CARES Act were misspent. The increased unemployment benefits clearly benefited the people most directly impacted by COVID-19 and helped them maintain their families and housing through difficult economic challenges. The one major improvement opportunity to this program is that people on unemployment should never make more than they did as employees. Although the stories of people refusing to return to work because they would make less than being unemployed were likely overblown, this was a significant issue and is yet another sign of how poorly designed and implemented the CARES Act was.

Good Tightroper Policy is Good COVID Policy

Despite its flaws, the CARES Act was extremely popular. The general sentiment has been that any problems with the program should be overlooked because it had to be created and implemented so quickly. How could anyone have seen a COVID-19 pandemic coming? It was the ultimate "black swan" event.

We are told that we should congratulate our Congress for moving so quickly to spend money on behalf of the people impacted.

This is at least partly true. Other than Bill Gates, Albert Camus, and a whole lot of science fiction writers, very few people saw anything like this coming. Since previously hyped "plagues" like SARS, swine flu, and Ebola never took hold in the US, it was easy to think we would never face an epidemic.

However, while this pandemic brought on an unprecedented health crisis in the US, the economic toll was all too commonplace. In fact, as far as Tightropers are concerned, COVID-19 is just a more severe case of what they deal with regularly—financial instability.

Tightropers know they can face financial stress from an increasing variety of reasons. Their employer may need to downsize or even go out of business due to competition or regulatory change. They may have health problems or need to leave the workforce to take care of aging parents. Or they may deal with any one of the innumerable unexpected expenses that drain savings and put pressure on families.

One of the reasons that Tightropers managed through the COVID-19 crisis as well as they have is that they learned long ago to be agile and respond quickly to change—often more smoothly than the Safely Stable. And as data from the Center for the New Middle Class shows, despite the unparalleled disruption from COVID-19, Tightropers quickly adjusted to the "new normal" and felt no less secure financially than before the pandemic.

CHART 4.5. Percentage Who Report Feeling Financially Insecure[15]

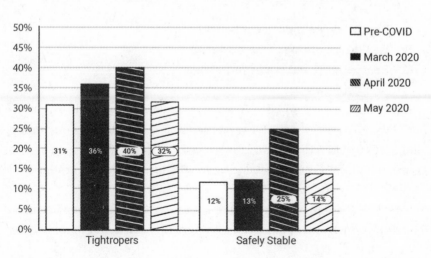

We should not view the economic turmoil of COVID-19 as a one-time event. Rather, we should treat it as an example of just how unstable our financial lives have become—in particular for Tightropers. Once a vaccine for COVID-19 is developed, we can't afford to reinsert our heads in the sand and hope for the best. Instead, we need to commit to policies that anticipate periods of income instability and help Tightropers successfully manage through them.

We need policies that are cost-effective, laser-targeted, and well-administered to avoid waste and fraud. Unfortunately, very few of the programs created by the CARES Act fit this definition. As a country, we should commit to a new generation of efficiently run programs for all Americans facing unemployment that can be scaled up if and when we have further pandemics or other "black swan" macroeconomic disasters.

Why wait for a catastrophe like COVID to ease the financial stress Tightropers feel when they face income instability? Knowing that job loss and job change are a regular life event for more than a hundred million Americans, we need to ensure that families can smoothly transition between jobs and even careers.

Later in the book I present a full list of policies and private sector innovations that can make a powerful difference in the lives of Tightropers. However, COVID highlighted the fact that Tightropers need—at the very least:

A.   **Improved unemployment benefits**
B.   **Healthcare during unemployment**
C.   **Rent support and credit forbearance**

If these programs had been in place, they could have been seamlessly (and far more cost-effectively) expanded as a result of rising unemployment. This would have avoided the excesses of the CARES Act and given people the support they needed to negotiate through the uncertainties of the COVID-19 pandemic.

Note that these programs are all meant to address economic hardship felt by individuals and families. This is where the pain is and should be the place to start.

As a businessperson I have sympathy for the thousands of businesses that go under as a result of a pandemic or any other event that changes competitive dynamics or market demand. However, except in rare cases, that money is best spent directly on American families.

How to Flatten the Curve of Income Instability and Economic Hardship

The CARES Act, despite its flaws, would have been a good solution for a very short epidemic. If we had gotten a vaccine quickly and a "V" shaped recovery we would have moved on as if nothing had happened.

But that's not how things played out and we've all come to realize that we may face future pandemics and economic crises. We're going to have to live with this uncertainty—the same way that Tightropers have been living with it for decades.

The COVID-19 pandemic taught the world a wide variety of new epidemiological concepts including the idea of "flattening the curve" of an epidemic. This means that rather than let a contagion run its course through a population uncontrolled, public policy measures can slow the spread which will allow the healthcare system to better manage the crisis. The goal of flattening the curve isn't necessarily to reduce the number of infected people, but rather to allow the healthcare system to keep up and not be overwhelmed.

We need to apply the same concept to the ongoing challenges facing Tightropers. We can't realistically stop income instability, but we can "flatten the curve" for impacted families so they can reorient and retool to get back on track.

COVID-19 was a wake-up call to a nation that wasn't paying attention to the changing economy that created over 100 million Tightropers. By becoming more aware of our vulnerability to events outside of our control, we should be able to come together to support Tightropers.

SECTION 2

Getting Started on the Tightrope

5

STARTING OUT...STRUNG OUT

Starting out on the Tightrope undermines lifelong financial security

- The traditional paths to financial success are no longer working for Tightropers.
- Americans in their twenties and thirties have lower income and wealth than earlier generations at the same age and they have been disproportionally impacted by the economic impacts of the Great Recession and COVID-19.
- Fear of eroding social security benefits fuel Tightropers' sense of financial insecurity.

ave worked hard to follow in his parents' footsteps. He went to college and started adult life in a great city, but even with two jobs, he's living paycheck to paycheck. It's hard for him to see a way off the Tightrope when even minor surprises—like getting paid at a different time of the month—cause financial stress.

I grew up in an upper-middle-class family in Los Angeles. My father was a nuclear chemist and my mom was a lawyer—pretty unusual for the 1970s! I mostly focused on going to the beach and surfing the waves and stuff.

There was never a question of whether I was going to college. It was a given. I think my parents would probably have killed me if I didn't go to college. So I rebelled by going as far from LA as possible—all the way to the east coast. Not exactly cheap, though. Had to take on more student debt than I'd like.

I'm living in Los Angeles now and working two jobs. I'm a teacher as well as a substitute teacher. The substitute teacher job is relatively good pay, but the catch is that sometimes I work five days a week and sometimes it's only one or two days a week. That means a lot of ups and downs for my income.

The other job is full time but the pay doesn't really cover the basics. Los Angeles is expensive!

I got a new job that I like but I guess I was spoiled getting paid every week at my old job. Since the new job is paid every other week instead of every week it's been hard to manage my finances. You know—rent is due on the first and they won't wait too long before they get unhappy—but I'm not getting paid until the twentieth. My money was misaligned and a lot of things were being paid slowly and causing me a lot of late fees.

Everyone knows the recipe for financial success in the US. Move away from home, go to college, get a steady job, and buy a house. What if I told you that for an increasing number of Americans like Dave, this has become a recipe for life on the Tightrope?

An unholy stew of student debt, job instability, and the high cost of living in the cities with the best jobs start off young adults in a financial hole. Millennials—today's 20- and early 30-somethings—must first climb to neutral financial ground before they can accelerate to the major milestones widely recognized to build long-term wealth: a career with reliably rising income, homeownership, and savings for the long term. Each of these factors might be surmountable alone, but the convergence of five-figure debt, flat earnings, and a cost of living that saps economic momentum is overwhelming for a large percentage of young Americans.

Because Tightropers like Dave start their adult lives with debt and high fixed costs (such as housing, car loan payments, cell phone bills, etc.), it takes a tremendous amount of financial discipline and/or luck to build any sort of financial safety net for the future. This leaves them extremely vulnerable to the sort of unexpected expenses and income swings that young adults are prone to.

It won't get easier as they age. Starting life on the Tightrope crystallizes financial fragility as the norm. Since almost every decision from real estate to romance is constrained by a credit score and credit history, it is becoming increasingly perilous to balance on the Tightrope while chasing dreams.

By traditional standards, Millennials—the approximately seventy-five million Americans born between 1980 and 1996—have followed the guidelines for success that worked in the past. They are far and away the most educated Americans ever. Nearly 90% of Americans now graduate high school (the highest number ever recorded),[1] and of those, 70% go on to enroll in college the year they graduated.[2] To put it in perspective, in 1980, when I graduated high school, only 50% of us went on to college.

Yet, young Americans are falling financially behind previous generations. Millennials make 20% less than Baby Boomers did at the same age and have half the assets. Adjusted for inflation, Baby Boomers earned an average of $50,910 whereas Millennials earn only $40,589. Early earnings set the stage for lifetime earnings, so this represents a major shift backwards in the financial prospects for young Americans.[3]

CHART 5.1. Erosion in Generational Wealth—Millennials vs Boomers

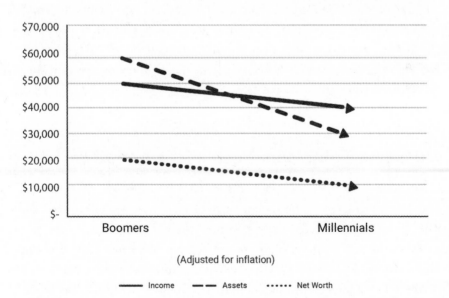

(Adjusted for inflation)

——— Income   — — Assets   ••••• Net Worth

Wealth creation is similarly stunted for Millennials. Their accumulated assets (that is, the sum of the value of an individual's bank accounts, retirement funds, life insurance policies, annuities, trusts, vehicles, real estate, and business equity) is less than $30,000 compared to more than $60,000 for Boomers at the same age (adjusted for inflation). To make matters worse, Millennials also have more debt than Boomers. As a result, Millennials have barely $10,000 in average net worth (accumulated assets minus liabilities)—56% less than Boomers at the same age.[4]

Tightropers and children of Tightropers are particularly impacted by this delay in wealth accumulation. Whereas Millennials with access to family financial resources are getting by, those coming from Tightroper families are finding it harder than ever to chart a path as an adult that leads away from the Tightrope.

This is a dangerous trend by any measure but is getting a lot worse in the wake of the COVID-19 pandemic as millions of young Tightropers delay careers and erode savings. Even before the devastating economic impact of the COVID-19 pandemic, the Social Security Administration estimated that by 2034, Social Security won't be able to pay out full benefits.[5] According to Alicia Munnell, Director of the Center for Retirement Research at Boston College, any solution that would rectify its finances will require more taxes and more benefit cuts—all coming out of the pockets of younger workers.[6]

Younger Tightropers are painfully aware of the crisis with Social Security. In fact, more than 80% of Americans between 18 and 29 believe Social Security benefits will either be reduced or nonexistent when they retire, according to Pew Research.[7]

Millennial Tightropers Need a New Narrative

Unfortunately, Millennials get a bad rap. They are widely perceived as lazy and unable to control their spending habits. Nineteen-dollar avocado toast should not be an indictment of an entire generation.

The truth is that Millennials are not the delicate snowflakes they are made out to be. More than any other generation, they have studiously followed the traditional paths to financial stability and responsible adulthood. But for them, these paths have led to unaffordable debt, job instability, and a lifetime on the financial Tightrope. In fact, they have a good claim to be the unluckiest generation ever, given that they had to deal with the twin crises of the Great Recession when they entered the workforce and COVID-19 just as their careers were getting into gear in their 30s.[8]

In a perfect world, twenty-somethings would start off their adult life with a leg up. They would be able to decide whether or not to attend college without taking on suffocating levels of debt. There would be a wide variety of stable, entry-level jobs for college graduates as well as for those with technical degrees and for people who choose to enter the workforce immediately after high school. These jobs would provide exciting early work experiences and mentoring to get young workers ready for long, satisfying careers. And there would be plenty of affordable "starter" homes that would appreciate rapidly, building long-term wealth.

In this perfect world, young people would be able to shake free from the early financial and career mistakes that we all make. The credit reporting and lending infrastructure would be quick to help them rebuild. And it would be easy to put away money every month—and not touch it—in order to build a retirement nest egg.

But we don't live in a perfect world.

Increasingly, the majority of young Americans struggle with their finances from the moment they leave home as adults and find it difficult to climb down from the Tightrope and achieve financial stability. In a post–COVID-19 world with high unemployment and wide-scale disruption of entire industries such as transportation, hospitality, and energy, this is going to get a lot worse. We are likely to have an entire generation that finds it cruelly difficult to get jobs that can lead to fulfilling careers and economic security.

According to the Financial Health Network, financial health derives from eight key elements such as spending less than one's income, paying bills on time, carrying manageable debt, having a prime credit score, and having sufficient savings. Their research found that only 9% of Americans between the age of eighteen and twenty-five were "financially healthy," shifting to 24% for those between twenty-six and thirty-five. But that still leaves the majority of twenty-somethings in Tightroper territory: 78% of adults younger than twenty-five were "not thriving" financially, and that decreased only to 57% as they entered their thirties.[9]

A study released in 2019 by Age Wave and Merrill Lynch[10] found that Millennials face the type of financial pressures that used to land in middle age:

- 82% say that their overriding financial concern is to make more money.
- 69% fear that they are missing out on life aspirations, in part due to financial responsibilities.
- 60% define "financial success" not in terms of career or wealth, but by being debt-free.

Can young adults bootstrap their way to financial stability? It's hard to see how. For many of them, student debt was a form of bootstrapping their futures, and it backfired. Simply earning more is not a guarantee of building savings and pulling free from the debt: The Financial Health Network found that while 85% of households with less than $60,000 in annual income were "not financially healthy," so were 50% of households with incomes of $100,000 or more.[11] This widespread economic frustration is fueling political unrest and resentment in young Americans and is on a path to get worse.

Hope for Future Generations of Tightropers

Despite the challenges, many young Tightropers remain hopeful and buoyant. And some are rejecting the traditional wisdom that has trapped their peers on the Tightrope.

Shannon, twenty-nine, views her history of moving from one retail job to another every couple of years as a series of experiments that have clarified what she really wants in a career. Once she figured out what she was good at and what she liked, she plotted a plan to finish her college education with focus… and minimal debt. She currently manages the morning shift at a suburban outpost of a national coffee shop chain.

I've been working since I was a teenager, and I've been living on my own since I was twenty-one. I bought my first car, on my own, when I was twenty-four. My parents raised me to be self-sufficient. Now that I'm with a company that offers tuition reimbursement, I'm starting college. I'm on track for my goals of having a family. And what I need isn't credit cards. It's credit when I need it, on terms that build my credit score instead of tearing it down.

It's easy for people to say, oh, if you need a little loan, ask your family. But it's not realistic to think that you'll have family to rely on. I've learned a lot about budgeting and money management. It actually is motivating me to achieve my career goals of finishing my degree and moving to a professional job.

Like so many Tightropers, Shannon is fiercely independent and takes accountability for her financial decisions. She doesn't want welfare; she wants a fair shot at financial wellness and stability.

We need to recognize that the world has changed dramatically and that we need new solutions and guidelines to get people like Shannon started out in life without the constant overhang of student debt, lack of savings, and high living expenses. We owe it to the next generation of Americans to get them on the path to financial stability right from the start.

6

COLLEGE—A LEG UP
OR A STEP BACKWARDS?

The old rules for success aren't working anymore

- College education is increasingly leading to lifelong debt rather than financial success.
- Loan forgiveness isn't a realistic solution—instead, we need new educational models and innovative ways to pay for it.
- Employers need to eliminate excessive credentialing for entry-level jobs that drive high levels of student debt.

Becky was excited about going to college, but after the first few years she ended up with far more debt than she realized. Now she's trying to get that under control.

I recently had to put school on hold for a year and work two jobs to make up for all of the debt I had accumulated. I just couldn't deal with all of that hanging over my head!

I am still paying on it, but trying to get it to a manageable level. Hopefully as I continue to work, I can get this reduced as much as possible, and continue with my education online, which is a lot cheaper.

The keys to success right now for me are prayer, meditation, and just taking a day or two for self-care every once in a while.

Until recently, college was considered a no-brainer. College started graduates on a path to economic success by giving them access to top jobs. Young people could expect to pull free from student debt—if they had any at all—and quickly amass the resources and momentum to build wealth for lifelong economic independence. This works when strong job prospects and expected earnings justify student debt and allow borrowers to pay it back quickly.

Student debt no longer pays off so easily. It is a financial drag on people in their twenties and thirties that makes it difficult to build financial independence and stability. This emerged as one of the key issues in the 2020 presidential race. In fact, one of the leading democratic contenders, South Bend, Indiana Mayor Pete Buttigieg, revealed that he and his husband have "six-figure student debt." Could he one day become the first Tightroper President?

It's time to question the assumption that traditional college is always the best path forward for high school graduates.

Americans have been told for decades that college is the key to lifetime success, and they listened. The number of college graduates skyrocketed, from barely 20% of all twenty-five- to twenty-nine-year-olds in 1980, to almost 35% by 2010. Women and Blacks, in particular, heard the message. The share of women and Blacks with a bachelor's degree or higher nearly doubled over the same period.

This rapid growth in college degrees following the Great Recession has been celebrated in many circles but the downsides are overlooked. While we have more college graduates, we also have more people who attempt college and don't graduate. In fact, almost 45% of college students don't graduate in six years or less—most of them taking on student debt with nothing to show for it.

Sadly, this situation is most acute for Blacks. Since more than 60% will not graduate within six years, the increased college entrance rates have actually resulted in worse financial outcomes for millions, creating unnecessary debt and career delays for a generation of recent high school graduates.

While it's certainly true that the US college education system is the best in the world, that doesn't mean it is a good choice for most Americans. For those from wealthy families who don't have to worry about student debt, college can be an exciting period that yields lifelong learning and connections. And for some careers, it is an essential stepping stone. But with the rapidly increasing cost of education, it can leave students saddled with debt for decades. Adjusted for inflation, tuition costs are up nearly 1500% since 1980. As a result, about 70% of college students must now borrow to cover the cost of their education.[1]

CHART 6.1. Six-Year College Outcomes by Race and Ethnicity[2]

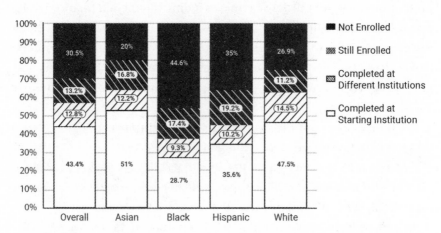

Student debt is probably the most sympathetic of all consumer debt. You'd have to be pretty hard-hearted to condemn an ambitious, bright teenager for not "investing in yourself" by way of borrowing for their education. After all, the rationale for student debt—originally, at least—was that college graduates earned so much more than those without degrees that the cost of the debt was easily repaid by higher income.

That assumption is shredding in the gears of a rapidly shifting economy and the realization that just as you pay off debt from college, twenty years after the fact, you might find yourself expected to take on another round of student debt to fund a midlife career shift. It appears that the return on a college degree is diminishing while the half-life of compounding student debt is increasing, creating more Tightropers than ever before.

But on an even more fundamental level, starting out with debt levies a psychological and cultural burden. The purported freedom of your twenties is dampened by the requirement to feed the debt machine. Instead of being footloose and free to try out different jobs and locales until they find the right fit, many Tightropers find their options curtailed by the need to stick with a well-paying job (or two).

The college graduating class of 2019 is starting adult life with an average of $30,000 in student debt. Adjusted for inflation, this is three times the debt load of the average student in the early 1990s.[3]

That $30,000 is much more daunting for a teacher than it is for a computer science major. Starting salaries for teachers average less than $40,000,[4] while a classmate who majors in computer science can expect to make nearly twice that—about $75,000—at her first job. Ironically, teaching is one of the few careers where a traditional college curriculum provides essential training.

It's no surprise that about 44% of Millennials who have student debt say that their college education wasn't worth it.[5]

In fact, one study by Third Way found that for many college degrees, the likelihood of getting a financial return on the cost over your entire life is about the same as a coin toss—and that's assuming you actually graduate. For those who don't graduate, almost no one receives adequate financial value for their investment in time and money.

CHART 6.2. Likelihood of Financial Benefit from College by Major[6]

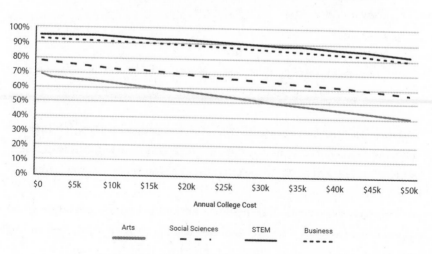

But what about all of those studies that show how much more people make with a college degree? That's certainly true, but it could be argued that this is due more to excessive credentialing by Human Resources departments than the educational impact of college. As a society, we should ask ourselves, Why is it acceptable that so many talented and capable Tightropers without a college degree are excluded from the vast majority of white-collar entry-level positions?

Our culture's excessive optimism about college education is no longer well-founded. We need to reinvent college programs for an unstable world, develop alternative funding approaches to student debt, and provide better career options for those who opt out of college.

How Tightropers Deal with Student Debt

According to a study by the Center for the New Middle Class, Tightropers (and children of Tightropers) deal with college decisions and student debt differently than wealthy families.[7]

Key findings include:

- Students from Tightroper households are more likely to attend public, community, or junior colleges.
- They are more likely to live at home.
- They are significantly more likely to say that financial aid affected their choice of schools.
- They are extremely reliant on financial aid, as nine out of ten will use some form of financial assistance to cover college expenses.

Unsurprisingly, access to financial aid is critical for the children of Tightropers because so many of them come from households with fluctuating incomes where their parents' financial situation is precarious and often burdened with high levels of debt.

This data suggests that Tightropers and their families are aware of the high costs of college and are attempting to get the benefits of a college education while limiting the economic risks. However, even this level of caution isn't enough to ward off severe financial downsides for many Tightropers who attend college.

Reinventing College for Tightropers

Traditional college programs are increasingly disconnected from the real world that students will join after graduating. Perhaps it's time to reevaluate our views on the relative merits of traditional colleges vs for-profit colleges. It turns out that there is a lot that traditional colleges can learn from for-profit institutions.

Kathy Boden Holland is one of the most talented business leaders I know. She managed some of Elevate's most successful products, then made a bold career transition to become President of Adtalem Global Education's Medical and Healthcare Group, formerly DeVry Education. She is now applying the deep understanding of Tightropers she learned by lending to them in her new role as a higher education leader.

Precisely because Adtalem is for-profit, Kathy is hyperfocused on ensuring that students get a return on their investment. She believes that "every dollar we spend may actually be borrowed by one of our students, so if we don't think it is worth it to them to borrow money for something, then we should really consider whether or not we're spending it the right way." Can you imagine a traditional college president saying that?

Here are some of the innovations Kathy and her team have introduced that all colleges can learn from.

Focus on Both Skills and Mindset for Success

At Adtalem, Kathy is pushing beyond simply providing subject matter training. Her goal is that her Tightroper graduates will be prepared to succeed in the real world, not just the classroom. Her challenge is particularly acute in this area since, as she says, "Harvard Medical School only takes high scoring students so they are essentially presorted for success, while we are taking students that may have struggled with school or have non-academic hurdles that impact their studies."

One of the programs that Adtalem provides is called "MERP" (Medical Education Readiness Program). It's a semester that is offered to certain borderline medical school applicants to prepare them for the rigors of the full program and help them "increase persistence." Kathy says that "what is fascinating about the program is that although the students are generally in the bottom quintile of admitted applicants, they are actually more likely to graduate than the entire medical program on average."

Additionally, they try to make sure students are "practice-ready." According to Kathy, "it's not enough to have students memorize the ten things they need to know. They also need to be able to go into situations with real people and real ambiguity and make good decisions. If we don't ensure that students are practice-ready, then six months after they start their first job they may leave because it's simply too overwhelming for them."

This suggests an important opportunity for both colleges and employers. By expanding the mission for education and training programs beyond the traditional curriculum, they can get Tightropers "practice-ready" for their jobs and help them learn "persistence," which can deliver lasting benefits for new generations of Tightropers.

Create Close Partnerships with Employers

Banfield is a large chain of veterinary hospitals that works very closely with Adtalem to gain access to top students. "On any given day, Banfield is trying to hire over 1,000 people in various roles," Kathy told me. "Successful recruiting is the key to their growth. As a result, we bring them in to get to know our students literally from orientation on through to graduation. They start recruiting from the moment the students walk in the door and they connect with students to provide opportunities like fellowships along the way. And our students get to know them before they commit to taking a job."

Students need a smooth transition between college and work-life and employers need a consistent pipeline of high-quality young workers—why doesn't every college commit to this level of interaction and integration with employers? Instead, they tend to put off recruiting activities until nearly graduation.

Increase Transparency and "Skin in the Game".

Although it's somewhat controversial in liberal arts departments at traditional colleges, it should be noncontroversial to people concerned about the financial impact of student debt to require all colleges (traditional as well as for-profit) to provide potential students with critical information such as graduation rates and the postgraduation salaries based on a given major. In 2019, the Department of Education significantly expanded its College Scorecard to do just this. The tool now includes information on nearly 6,000 degree and nondegree postsecondary education options with comprehensive data on graduation rates and student loan debt by field of study.

However, it's not enough to simply provide generic information and hope for the best. Colleges need to be more proactive in helping students avoid unnecessary debt.

A big part of what has driven up student debt is the increased time it now takes most students to graduate. Less than twenty percent of public university students now graduate with a degree in four years.[8] At Adtalem, Kathy says that they try to help students understand the linkage between time to graduate and total debt. They actually provide financial counseling to students so they realize how much more money they will make over their lives if they graduate and start working earlier.

Adtalem has taken even further steps to increase their accountability for student success. In particular, with MERP, if you don't successfully complete the program, they give you your money back. If only every college offered a money-back guarantee!

Create Alternatives to Student Debt

Over forty-four million people owe student debt. Total US student debt is now over $1.5 trillion.[9] Barely more than a decade ago, in 2006, this number was less than $500 billion. This has created a crisis of unaffordability and is a significant driver of the growth in Tightropers since the Great Recession.

In many ways, easy access to government-guaranteed student loans has removed incentives for colleges and universities to control costs and ensure loan affordability. Certainly, traditional colleges seem to have lost their focus on the educational and career success of their students. They spend 25% less on professors and core instruction than in the past[10] and instead have invested in a variety of unrelated student services such as athletic programs and luxurious housing.

This may be fine for the offspring of well-to-do families for whom college is a fun break between high school and "the real world," but for the average American Tightroper who will take on debt to attend college, it is scandalous. In fact, it is expected that as many as 40% of students who borrow today will eventually default.[11] Tragically, this debt can't be eliminated by bankruptcy and can lead to wages being garnished and credit damaged for years.

This growing financial crisis has led to increasing calls for free college for all and some have even proposed full loan forgiveness for all student debt. The astronomical cost of these proposals—$79 billion annually for free college tuition[12] and $2.2 trillion for student debt forgiveness[13]—make it unlikely that this will ever become a reality.

Furthermore, any loan forgiveness for student debt will benefit the affluent far more than Tightropers. Students from families earning over $114,000 take out loans twice as large as students from lower incomes.[14] And of course, the people with the largest student debt are often those who received the most value, including doctors, lawyers, and other people with advanced professional degrees.

Although government programs have struggled to make a dent in the situation, innovation from the private sector is showing the potential to change the way people borrow for college.

One of the newest ideas is called an "income share agreement," or ISA. Instead of a traditional student loan that requires the borrower to make fixed payments over a fixed schedule, payments on ISAs are based on the income the student makes after college. That is, they are an "equity" investment in the student rather than a loan. If a student is unemployed (or chooses to go on a lengthy vacation) they pay nothing. However, if a student is a particularly high earner after college, they may pay quite a bit more than they would with a standard loan.

Purdue is the most prominent college to use ISAs, but it is expected that at least 100 American universities and technical schools will begin offering them in the next few years.[15] These programs typically tailor the payment terms to fit the educational major of the student. That is, an ISA for a student in computer engineering that is expected to lead to a high-paying job will be required to pay a smaller percentage of their salary over a shorter period than a liberal arts major who will pay more for longer.

CHART 6.3. Growth in ISA Originations in the US[16]

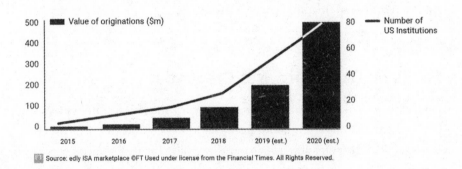

The ISA concept is appealing since it allows people who get a lot of value from their degrees to pay more, while the ones who don't realize the financial results pay quite a bit less (or even nothing at all). This fits with our society's view of fairness, and if offered by colleges directly, would drive more accountability for educational outcomes.

Bipartisan federal legislation (a rare concept these days) was introduced in 2019 by Republicans Todd Young and Marco Rubio and Democrats Mark Warner and Chris Coons. The proposed new rules would allow ISA contracts that are quite a bit more onerous than those typically available today (as much as 7.5% of income for up to thirty years!) and are an indication that this alternative to student debt is being taken very seriously.

The challenge, of course, is "adverse selection." The people who know they are unlikely to repay the money are the most likely to sign up for it. For instance, trust fund children who may take years before they seriously pursue their careers or those who expect to work at low-income nonprofits may gravitate to these products, making them less profitable over time for investors.

Despite the likelihood that some people will game the system, ISAs are an exciting innovation with tremendous potential. They may lead to better outcomes for young Tightropers and provide incentives for universities to ensure that students graduate and see the results of their studies and hard work. However, there are numerous issues to be resolved. In particular, how will people feel when Deep Learning computer models are used to predict lifetime income potential for seventeen-year-olds as a way to price the ISA offers? From a regulatory perspective, and even more so from a moral one, this will be concerning.

Focus on Capability, Not Credential

It's unfair to place the entire responsibility for the student debt crisis on schools. Excessive credentialing for entry-level positions has exacerbated the situation. It seems like every job these days needs a degree or some sort of credential or license. This has become an unfair structural barrier to success for millions of Americans. In Texas, even working in a nail salon requires 600 hours of coursework and training![17] And a college degree is assumed for most white-collar and information-worker jobs these days—whether they are needed or not. This creates an unnecessary and expensive hurdle to higher-paying careers and is why so many Tightropers feel the need to take on crippling student debt.

Fortunately, this is changing. Many leading companies are removing the requirement for a four-year degree. Even Google, famously known for its strict focus on elite college success and grade point averages, no longer requires a college degree. Other top technology companies such as Apple and Netflix have joined in and recognize that a successful career—even one demanding high coding skills—doesn't rely on an expensive college education.

Additionally, many large employers now offer tuition reimbursement programs, including lower-wage employers such as Starbucks and Chipotle.[18] However, the problem is that these programs are only tax-free to employees up to $5,250 per year. This is an unacceptably low level that minimizes the potential use of these programs. Raising the limit could dramatically improve the financial stability of young Tightropers without significantly impacting the federal budget.

Celebrate All Choices—Not Just College

College graduation is a staple cliché: the black gowns and mortarboards, the proud parents, the still-damp diploma. High school counselors, the educational-industrial complex, and the media have pronounced that this is the only way to prosperity, and that once you graduate you "have it made." As a result, high schools tend to give the greatest accolades to those who are moving on to (often high-cost) college educations.

Where's the celebration for students heading to technical school, career programs, and learn-on-the-job employment? One Virginia school system created that milestone[19] with "Career and Technical Letter-of-Intent Signing Day." Students get a photo op and congratulations for starting on a path that is just as legitimate—and often more financially rewarding—than four years at college. What a wonderful way to support the diverse educational and life decisions that Tightropers make!

We need more moments like these.

7

NO SUCH THING AS A STEADY JOB

How to unrig the gig for Tightropers

- "Side Hustles" are becoming increasingly essential in this fast-changing economy.
- Outdated assumptions of labor and jobs block needed policy initiatives.
- New financial products and services can help young "gig workers" build savings and manage through unexpected changes in income and expenses.

Jake is focused on building his career. He has changed jobs a few times already to try to move up the ladder. But it's not always a straightforward journey. Sometimes it feels like "one step forward, two steps back."

Recently, I changed jobs. I like the new job, but I didn't realize how much the commute would cost. $350 a month! Which needed to be paid before I got my first paycheck.

I got through the pay gap of old and new jobs by cashing out vacation days when I left my previous job and not taking time off between the switch. But I'm still pretty tight right now. I'll probably need to get another job so I can put some money away.

A key traditional requirement for financial success and independence has always been a steady job. Getting on the first rung of the career ladder—preferably with a top-tier company—was historically a critical objective for young Americans.

However, companies no longer provide the kind of long-term employment they once did, and young Tightropers like Jake know it. According to a study by Deloitte, more than 70% of Millennials expect to change jobs within the next five years. For Gen Z, the number is 88%.[1]

No one expects the return of lifetime employment anytime soon. Those days are long past, and ongoing technology-driven disruptions—not to mention the macroeconomic impact of events such as the COVID-19 pandemic—are making any type of employment seem increasingly fragile.

Scrappy Tightroper Millennials have embraced this new world and have fueled the growth of Gig Economy apps like Fiverr, TaskRabbit, and Upwork, as well as Uber, Lyft, and Instacart. Tightropers recognize they can't afford to wait for the "perfect job" that will last a lifetime. They use these apps to both supplement traditional job income and help bridge between jobs.

"Side Hustles," as these jobs are often called, used to be only for desperate people who couldn't get a "real" job. For many young Tightropers, especially, they are now a normal component of work life and in many ways a lifesaver. They provide additional cash flow to cover unexpected expenses and help add to savings. And when people suffer job loss (or even reduced hours), gig work helps young Tightropers manage while looking for their next job.

Younger Tightropers are reporting a fundamental shift from traditional assumptions about work and employment. More than 80% of Millennials and Gen Zers would consider joining the Gig Economy either instead of full-time employment or to supplement full-time employment.[2] This overwhelming recognition of the attractiveness and/or necessity of gig work suggests that younger Americans feel that traditional jobs aren't paying enough and that they may go away.

In addition to extra cash flow, Side Hustles can provide psychological benefits. According to one study, self-employed workers report higher work satisfaction than those with traditional jobs, and half of people with multiple jobs state that it is for reasons besides financial necessity.[3] Hence workers, as well as employers, are driving the move toward a Gig Economy.

Unfortunately, gig work brings financial complications for young Tightropers along with the increased cash flow. Part-time jobs and platform-based gigs (such as Uber, etc.) both yield much less net income, after taxes and the cut that the platform takes, than workers anticipate. And it takes superhuman self-discipline to direct all of that "extra" income to paying down debt or to savings.

Side Hustles have none of the stabilizing benefits of traditional full-time employment. They don't come with healthcare, they don't contribute to your 401(k), and they don't withhold for state and federal taxes. Although they provide cash flow, they push a tremendous amount of financial responsibility back to the individual Tightroper and make it hard to put money away for emergencies and retirement. This is a terrible burden to put on hardworking young Americans.

Rethinking Labor Policies in a Gig Economy

We need to rethink our perspective on gig work. We can't afford to view it as simply a temporary situation in between "real" jobs. It is now a key component of our modern economy that has the potential to provide needed income for Tightropers at the same time that it further erodes their financial safety nets. Worker protections, tax codes, and the like are all structured on the outdated assumption of steady employment and income. Policymakers need to recognize the new reality for young Tightropers and help gig workers build financial stability in unstable times.

Part-time and contractor wages should come with automatic withholdings and automatic enrollment in IRAs to help Tightropers build essential nest eggs. Shifting from opt-in to opt-out for these plans would make a huge difference. My own experience as an employer was that far less than half of employees opted in to our 401(k) plan—even with a generous matching program. Once we shifted to opt-out, on the other hand, very few employees left the program, which helped them build savings with minimal perceived effort.

The current political narratives are largely unhelpful for solving this issue. This is not a situation where unions are the answer for protecting labor—these aren't the sort of long-term jobs that would make sense to unionize. Nor are laissez-faire policies adequate for the challenge. The structural changes that have created Tightropers and the gig economy aren't going away and will lead to an eventual economic crisis as younger Americans age and begin to retire.

We can't ignore the financial stress facing young gig workers—especially following the economic impacts of the COVID-19 pandemic. Policymakers and legislators need to listen to young Tightropers to find out what will make a difference in their lives and help them build for the future.

Innovation Opportunities and Imperatives

While new governmental policies are inevitably fraught with political discord and the potential for unanticipated consequences, providing better financial tools and services for Tightropers is far easier to achieve.

Banks should be leading the charge to help young Tightropers save and learn financial discipline, but they are at risk of being disrupted by upstart financial technology providers more in tune with our changing reality.

Banks are already losing to Fintech payment processors like PayPal, Venmo, Zelle, and Square for moving money. These new providers are making payments easier for fast-paced lives and many automate tax reporting for contractors and gig workers. PayPal, for one, generates 1099-K tax forms directly based on account transactions. However, they don't withhold for taxes and they don't help customers build savings.

Fortunately, new Fintech mobile apps are attempting to transform the way consumers—especially Millennial and Gen Z Tightropers—save for the future. Apps like Acorns, Chime, Digit, and Stash, among a host of other upstarts, have acquired tens of millions of customers by offering painless ways for Tightropers to build a cash cushion. Instead of traditional budgeting programs meant to shame people into putting aside part of their income each month, these apps focus on small withdrawals that don't create hardship for the customer, but over time generate real savings that can help keep the customer from having to use a payday lender if they have a financial emergency.

- **Acorns** saves with periodic withdrawals or by moving the spare change from transactions (to the nearest dollar amount) into an investment account rather than a savings account.
- **Chime** enables consumers to automatically save a percentage of their deposits and to round up transactions to the next dollar. For every purchase or bill paid with the Chime Visa Debit Card, the transaction is rounded up to the nearest dollar and the difference is transferred to the Automation Savings Account.
- **Digit** uses a complex algorithm to analyze upcoming income and bills, bank balance, and recent spending patterns. Every few days, it calculates a "safe to save today" amount and moves it to the Digit account.
- **Stash** offers "Smart-Stash," which automatically moves aside small amounts of money based on an analysis of customer transactions. Users can set a maximum transfer amount to ensure too much money doesn't get withdrawn.

These apps evidence a deep understanding of the Tightroper dilemma. Tightropers are aware that they need to save and budget for upcoming expenses, but the reality is that at the end of the month there just isn't much left to move into savings. By simplifying the process of saving and making it part of everyday purchases, these apps remove the pain and allow savings to build without any specific action or decision from the Tightroper.

For a traditional banker, the idea of moving extra change from transactions into a savings or investment account sounds absurd. However, for fast-paced, technically savvy Tightroper Millennials, it makes perfect sense. They don't want to be harangued by stodgy financial literacy programs and don't have the time to think about savings. They need financial providers that are "on their side" to do the work for them.

Fintech innovators are also providing technology-enabled short-term credit products designed with young Tightropers in mind. In recent years, there has been a rapid growth in new, low-cost financial technology offerings from what have become known as "challenger banks." These include companies such as Chime, MoneyLion, Dave, and Earn-In. All of these companies offer small-dollar credit that is particularly well-suited to the fast-paced needs of young gig workers. The credit that is available through these companies is typically no more than $100 and is repaid rapidly—usually on the customer's next payday.

Some examples of credit solutions from challenger banks that are designed for the needs of young Tightropers:

- **Chime:** $100 "SpotMe" loan that has no fee and is repaid from the next direct deposit.
- **Dave:** Up to $75 advance with no fee. Repaid from the next direct deposit.
- **EarnIn:** Gives customers access to wages that they have earned in the current pay cycle. Customers pay a "tip" rather than interest or fees and the advance is repaid from the next direct deposit.
- **MoneyLion:** Up to $250 "Instacash" advance with no fee that is repaid from the next direct deposit. Also, up to $500 "Credit Builder" low-cost loan, but only a portion of the loan proceeds are available to the customer—the rest are placed in a deposit account as collateral.

The financial needs of young gig workers are starting to gain the attention they deserve. In fact, Shaquille O'Neal, the basketball star, is backing a company called **Steady,** an "income-building" platform that provides young Tightropers in the gig economy with flexible, on-demand jobs and financial services that fit their needs—basically a job hub for gig workers.

As innovators listen to the needs of Tightropers and understand the size of the market opportunity, the kinds of products and services available to this growing but underserved demographic of Americans should improve.

8

MOVING AWAY FROM HOME

Hatching a nest egg or digging a money pit?

- Younger Americans are moving back home at record rates—is this a problem?
- Upfront housing costs drain savings just when Tightropers are most vulnerable.
- New models for housing young Tightropers are needed to increase flexibility in case of job changes and instability.
- Financial innovation to support the housing challenges of young Tightropers is an important opportunity.

larisse moved to Chicago after graduating college. However, the high cost of living and some big unexpected expenses impeded her plans of financial independence.

I love living in Chicago! But I could do without the high rent. Between that and high insurance premiums through my employer, it's killing me. And I had a car accident recently, so I had to get a loan to pay for that.

Now I'm working on my budgeting and trying to limit extra expenditures. Working extra hours occasionally, couponing, and only purchasing items during sales or liquidations. It's not a lot of fun.

It's hard not to feel for the hardworking, ambitious Millennial who sacrifices to go to a top school and gets a job in a big city, yet is so underwater financially that she can't possibly afford to save for the future.

And it's not because of excessive spending. The stereotype of the latte-drinking hipster may have some validity, but it's not the cause of financial hardships for most young Tightropers. Even those on the strictest budgets find it very difficult to build up any meaningful savings when they struggle with student debt, high living expenses, and unstable income.

The problem is in many ways cultural. America celebrates independence—starting with personal independence by moving out.

Increasingly, Millennial Tightropers don't buy (or can't afford) this definition of adult life. Rising housing costs and shrinking incomes and savings are causing young Tightropers to stay with their parents longer than previous generations.

CHART 8.1. Percentage of Young Americans Living at Home by Generation[1]

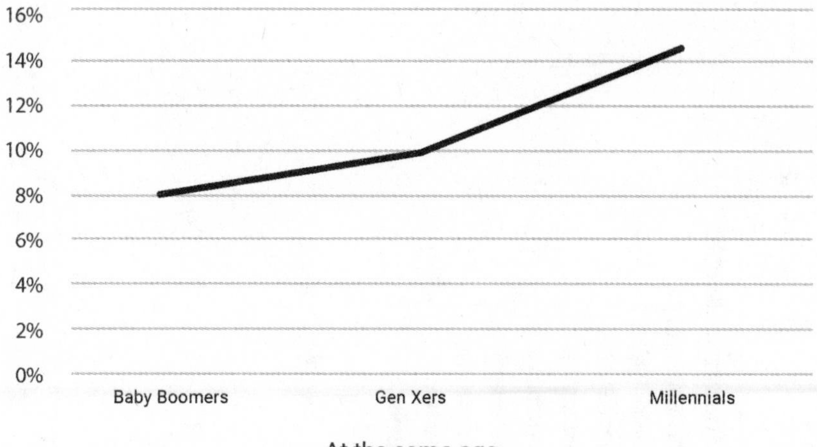

At the same age

About 15% of Millennials live with their folks, compared to 10% of Gen Xers when they were in their twenties, and about 8% of the first wave of Baby Boomers at the same age. The Millennial homeownership rate is eight percentage points lower than both Gen X and Baby Boomers at the same age.[2] Their famous perceived reluctance to shoulder the traditional responsibilities of adult life, including mortgages and families, is rippling throughout the entire economy, with major implications for housing, municipal planning, and the financial planning and investment industries.

This situation creates stress and embarrassment for Tightropers who view moving out as a crucial step toward being an adult. Brokerage company TD Ameritrade interviewed people between the ages of thirteen and twenty-six who reported that on average, they would be embarrassed to still live with their parents after age twenty-eight.[3]

Is this a problem that we need to solve?

For most Tightropers like Clarisse, the first economic shock of adulthood is paying rent. Just finding a place that will rent to a young person—in particular, one with a low credit score—is a frustrating challenge in many cities.

The average rent in the US has grown 36% over the past ten years, to $1,473 per month.[4] That increase is eating into the cash flow of Tightropers across the country.

However, the real story is how variable rent is between cities. Rents in the top coastal cities—the ones with the most jobs—are two to three times the average, while many midwestern cities cost half of the national average.

CHART 8.2. 1 Bedroom Rental Costs by City (Top 10 / Bottom 10)[5]

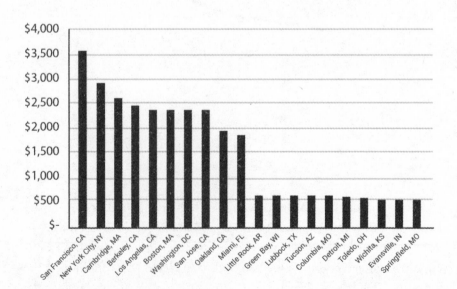

Trying to save money as a young Tightroper in a coastal city while build-ing a career is a Sisyphean challenge. The rule of thumb is that rent should be less than 30% of gross income. That means that people in San Francisco, for instance, would need to make $140,000 per year to afford the average rent of $3,500 per month.

Renting also carries high upfront costs. Between security deposits, first and last month's rent, and other costs for things like furniture, paint, moving assistance, etc., most young renters find their savings wiped out just to move in. This is the reason that many young Tightropers start rely-ing heavily on credit cards and personal debt. And to add insult to injury, in markets like New York City, they may also have to pay a broker's fee of up to two months' rent!

Nor is buying a house—even if you can afford it—the "safe" bet that it once was.

Freddie Mac is forecasting that home prices will grow by 3.6% in 2019 and 2.6% in 2020.[6] However, this is barely 1% more than annual inflation.[7]

And homeowning comes with a tremendous amount of fixed costs and unexpected expenses—exactly what can cause financial problems for young Tightropers.

For young Tightropers with limited savings and income volatility, home ownership can be one of the most deceptive and dangerous finan-cial decisions they can make. Homeownership locks in the cost of living and anchors the owner to one location. Millennials need flexibility and protection from outsized unexpected expenses. Carrying a mortgage in many cases is a foreclosure waiting to happen—we saw the results of this during the Great Recession and will see it again in the aftermath of the COVID-19 pandemic.

Cherishing Multi-Generational Living

In the US we expect people to move away from home as soon as possible, but that often leads to financial stress and eroded savings. The result of this financial pressure is the rise of Generation Boomerang, a term that describes the vast numbers of young Americans who are moving back home to live with their parents.

The social stigma of living with your parents after graduation is so well-known that it became the basis for a movie—the comedy *Failure to Launch* with Matthew McConaughey. In this new world of economic instability, is staying with parents such a terrible thing? Rather than being a cause for concern, this is actually a very smart financial choice that gives young people a chance to build up some savings.

In other countries, living with your parents until you're married isn't embarrassing at all. According to the Organization for Economic Development,[8] many other countries have much higher percentages of young people who live at home. In Italy, for instance, about 80% of adults up to twenty-nine-years old live at home.[9] This is not looked down upon. In fact, in many countries, children who move away from home quickly are seen as abandoning their families.

We need to rethink our cultural values, and congratulate parents and their adult children who continue to live together. Multigenerational living is an important ongoing investment by parents in the financial success of their children. And for young adults and their peers, it should be recognized as a positive sign that they are committed to starting adult life with as much savings as possible.

Affordable Housing in an Unaffordable World

Of course, this isn't the entire answer to the housing woes of young Tightropers—realistically they can't live with their parents forever. Work opportunities may not be close to home and parents may not be comfortable keeping their child in the house indefinitely. But the financial strains that come from owning a home or even renting an apartment today make it impossible for young adults to save for the future. We need housing solutions that are both more affordable and more flexible.

Remember WeWork? Similar to the way they pioneered coworking, they had plans to take on co-living with their WeLive brand. Unfortunately, when excessive growth and expenses caused them to implode spectacularly in 2019, these ideas became part of the wreckage. However, the concept has real value.

A project called **Haven** is trying to address this need in an extremely high-cost area—Venice Beach, California. Approximately 100 people live in the four townhouses that comprise Haven and each pay less than $1,000 a month. No one has a private room but rather each bedroom sleeps four people in individual sleeping pods. Real estate ideas like this one are notoriously hard to scale, but the explosion of coworking office space across the US proved it's possible.

Of course, with heightened sensitivity to potential infection from future pandemics, denser housing alternatives may be a hard sell. However, what is the alternative?

With the lack of affordable housing across the country, there is an important opportunity for developers to build a new type of co-living facility. These housing options will look very different from traditional apartment dwellings, but represent an alternative to the endless handwringing in the media and from government officials about the housing crisis. Realistically, the issue will never go away until we are willing to embrace radically new housing models such as co-living.

Financial Innovation
for Millennial Housing Problems

Every major US city struggles with a lack of sufficient affordable housing. It's unrealistic to assume this will be resolved overnight. Until then, we need new approaches to the way Tightropers finance and pay for housing.

There have been a number of start-ups focused on the financial needs of Millennial renters. Two examples, **Domuso** and **Till**, offer credit specifically for the purpose of either moving into an apartment or to avoid being evicted due to income shortfalls. They allow the customer to make payments over time when they don't have sufficient savings to cover the cost all at once. These products are priced far lower than alternative products like payday loans but are controversial.

Who could argue that helping people avoid being evicted is a bad thing? Apparently, lots of well-meaning consumer advocates, that's who. Criticisms of products like these are a classic example of letting perfect be the enemy of good. Unfortunately, financial services that appear to profit from the financial setbacks of others can seem predatory, even if they are better than the alternatives.

We're also beginning to see new paradigms for financing homeownership as well. A firm called **Haus** is turning the traditional world of home-buying upside down. Instead of waiting for people to slowly save for a down payment on a home, Haus "co-invests" most of the home's value, eliminating the need for a mortgage altogether. Ongoing monthly payments from the occupant allow them to increase their ownership over time (or lower it if they miss payments).

There are a lot of advantages of this model for both parties. For the co-investor, they get to invest in a sector of the market that has had strong historical appreciation without having to deal with the upkeep of the houses. And for the occupant, they get low upfront costs and strong protections against eviction.

Housing is an area that demands even more financial innovation. I recently got an apartment in Dallas to be close to my operations team and can relate to the pain of move-in expenses. Saving up for first and last month rent, a security deposit, and the host of additional moving expenses is a tremendous drain on the finances of cash-constrained young Tightropers. This is a huge business opportunity for financial innovators and investors to pursue.

SECTION 3

Tightropers in Midlife

9

MIDLIFE CRISES

When "life happens," working families face life on the Tightrope

- It isn't irresponsible spending in midlife that keeps most people on the Tightrope, but rather "responsible" spending.
- The main causes of financial stress in midlife are the rising costs of raising a family and the disruptive impact of career instability.
- One of the ways that Tightropers help preserve their balance is through credit, but that can quickly get out of control, resulting in a mountain of debt.

Antonio and Kelly have been together for over twenty years and have two children graduating from high school. They're closer than they have ever been. If life would just cooperate, they could get off the Tightrope.

We know what we should be doing financially at this point in our lives, but it's hard to stick with it. Things are going great, but the results aren't what we want.

I wish that the only thing I had to worry about was work. I love my kids—but they are a handful. My son had some troubles with the law a few years back and we had to pay to send him to military school. What a turnaround! He did really well, but it wasn't cheap. $30,000, but what was I going to do? I knew he just needed to get back on the right path.

A few years ago, my wife, Kelly, decided that enough was enough at the private school where she worked—it was grinding her down. I was happy that my job allowed her to quit and start her dream job—running her own ceramic studio and shop.

She's super-talented, so her ceramics are selling well—bringing in thousands each month. The only downside is that as a teacher she had affordable health insurance and regular retirement savings. That's harder to do while she's starting up the new business. Also, getting a kiln and renting a studio aren't free. It made things a struggle financially for a while.

Of course, that was exactly the time that our daughter had a skateboard accident. $8,000 in out-of-pocket medical expenses!

First things first—I'm taking care of my family's immediate needs before saving for retirement. But it got really bad when self-employment taxes caught me by surprise. Owing $72,000 to the IRS is pretty scary.

We thought about taking an early withdrawal from our retirement savings to pay it off, but fortunately our financial advisor talked us out of that. It would have cost so much in fees and penalties, and to be honest, I doubt we would have repaid that savings given everything else that we were facing.

So we refinanced our house. That got the IRS off our back and helped us pay off our credit card debt and medical expenses.

It has been a struggle, but now we're seeing our credit score come back up. I don't want to say how low it got, but it's currently 640. I think we can get it back up to 700 before long.

I have to say it's getting a bit tiring. I'd love to be able to manage my finances without these unexpected expenses. Don't get me wrong—I'm happy and proud that I can take care of my kids and wife—they are everything to me. But if you'd have told me when I was twenty-five that I'd be making $150,000 a year, I'd have thought I was set. Life hasn't turned out to be quite so simple.

Antonio and Kelly's story is typical. They are a hardworking and talented couple that understand how to manage their money, but their family comes first. And sometimes midlife events get in the way of that straightforward path toward retirement that we all dream of.

Midlife Is Crunch Time

When people reach their thirties and forties, they start to feel the pressure. It's when people have families and take on the financial responsibilities that come with raising children, including childcare, education, housing, and helping them grow and thrive. Roots are established in the community and families start feeling "settled."

And it's when individuals realize that if they are going to amass the resources for retirement, they'd better start saving and investing now, because they won't have much time to catch up if they wait until their fifties. That's a key reason that stress—in particular, financial stress—is at its peak in our midlife years.

CHART 9.1. Levels of Happiness and Stress by Age[1]

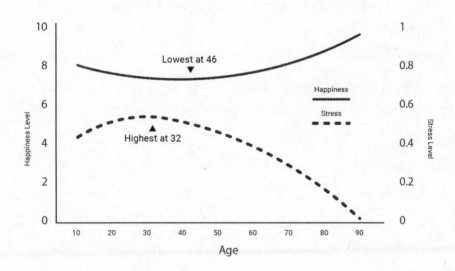

Millions of midlife Americans like Antonio and Kelly now find it difficult to live the American Dream of stability and financial independence. In a postindustrial world with accelerating disruption and transformation, no job is safe. We can no longer count on lifelong careers and are increasingly vulnerable to unexpected life events that are more destabilizing than ever before.

The COVID-19 pandemic is an extreme example of the type of curve-balls that life throws us every day. Entire industries have shut down and pushed millions of Americans into a level of financial instability that would have been thought impossible just months earlier during record employ-ment levels and stock market gains.

When "life happens" in your thirties and forties, it can quickly turn the prime of life into a lifetime of subprime financial stresses and strains.

The most critical financial concerns for Tightropers in their thirties and forties typically relate to children and marriage, career upheavals, and unmanageable credit. My conversations with Tightropers about their ex-periences with these issues have highlighted their remarkable resilience and optimism, but also the need for new policies and services to help them manage through challenging times and get back on their feet.

We need a new path for midlife Tightropers that leads them from the uncertainties of youth toward a safe retirement without having to sacrifice their families.

10

RAISING FAMILIES ON THE TIGHTROPE

The new Sophie's choice: children or a comfortable retirement?

- Child-rearing has become dramatically more expensive—the cost of raising a child is the same as what it takes to retire.
- Key financial strains include daycare and schooling—and costs continue well after high school.
- Employers need to be more flexible to support employees with children.

We all know that it's expensive to raise a child, but sometimes it's the little things that push young families over the edge. Janey, a security officer, was dealing with a difficult divorce and trying to make sure her kids had some stability in their lives as they moved into a new apartment.

> *I worked and saved to get our own apartment to get away from an abusive husband. The cat deposit was $400 per cat—can you believe that! However, after getting a protective order against my husband I couldn't think of asking the girls to give up their cats. And then Christmas came, and we ran into a real bind.*

More than ever before, having a child is an enormous financial burden. Unlike in the 1800s, when children helped reduce costs by working on the farm or in the family business, today's kids are a drain on family wealth and make it increasingly difficult for young families to save for retirement.

The most recent government figures suggest that raising a child born in 2015 to age eighteen will cost the average middle-income family nearly a quarter of a million dollars—$233,610, to be precise.[1]

This stunning figure includes expenses integrated into the household's overall cost of living, such as housing (because parents often feel the need to either purchase a house or increase the size of their house to accommodate children) and food, as well as costs that are specific to the child such as childcare and education. However, these estimated costs are exclusively out-of-pocket expenses and do not include any money that a parent forfeits by working less or not at all.

This is an astounding and daunting number. There is no doubt that most young couples would question their commitment to raising children if they realized the full financial burden. According to JP Morgan Asset Management, couples with a household income of $75,000 should have saved three times their income by age forty-five for retirement. This equals $225,000—about the cost of a single child![2] No wonder we have so many Tightropers with no savings for retirement.

CHART 10.1. Cost for Raising a Child vs Saving for Retirement

$234K — Cost of raising a child to age 18

$225k — Target for retirement savings by age 45

The cost of raising a child has grown dramatically over the years, but it has also changed in important ways. A family raising a Boomer in 1960 spent far more on items like clothing, food, and transportation. These lower costs are likely due to the mixed blessing of lower-cost chains such as Walmart and McDonald's. However, the amount spent on childcare and education (from 2% to 16%) and healthcare (from 4% to 9%) have skyrocketed.

No doubt the increases in the out-of-pocket expenses related to childcare and education stem from the rapid growth in the number of two-income families. In two-thirds of American families today, both parents work (93% of fathers and 72% of mothers with children at home are in the labor force).[3]

CHART 10.2. Change in Child-raising Costs—1960 vs 2015[4]

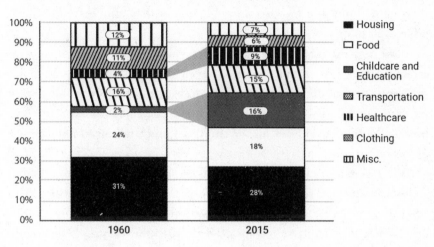

Parenting has become a thorny financial trap for those with limited resources. Dual income seems like a great solution, but even that has its downsides. As now-Senator, then-professor Elizabeth Warren outlined in her book, *The Two-Income Trap: Why Middle-Class Parents are Still Going Broke*,[5] midlife parents increase their earnings and their cost of living in tandem to try to afford the best schools and the most opportunities for their children. As we saw with Antonio and Kelly, parents often sacrifice their own savings and even their long-term financial stability to provide for their children.

The costs and sacrifices start early. Daycare and preschool costs can be incredibly stressful to families—both financially and psychologically. In some cases, the costs are so high that the additional job barely pays the costs of daycare. According to a survey by the New York Times and YouGov, nearly 60% of those polled said they experienced "very significant" or "somewhat significant" financial strain from preschool and daycare expenses.[6]

In addition, the reliance on preschool and daycare causes many devoted parents to feel guilty about leaving their children with others, which leads to even more spending in an attempt to reinforce their love for their children. As Janey highlighted earlier, we often use gift-giving to demonstrate our love, reward accomplishment, or help ease disappointments. For already-stretched Tightropers, rising to gift-giving occasions such as Christmas and birthdays can be rationalized as self-sacrifice ("I'll go without, but my kids won't"), even as they anticipate the inevitable debt hangover.

All of the costs we've discussed so far assume that the parents stay together. About 40% of first-time marriages will end in divorce—at a median duration of eight years. And divorces with children at home are particularly expensive. They cost an average of $19,200 (almost twice as much as a divorce without minor children) and drag on for an average of eleven months.[7]

And the costs of raising children don't stop at high school.

Lucy is a human resources specialist in an ophthalmology office. She has two grown children, one eight-year-old daughter, and four grandchildren aged from just a few months old to eight years old. Her family is the center of her life and she'd sacrifice anything to help them get ahead.

> As a mother you put your children first. You want to make sure they have the opportunity to pursue their goals in life and you want to be part of their successes. My son worked so hard to get into school up in Oregon, I couldn't have been more proud.
>
> We were already living paycheck to paycheck when this opportunity came up for him. I didn't realize how much it would cost, beyond the scholarships. The cost of getting him there, the books, the fees, the cost of traveling home for school break. I didn't realize all that. I had to make sure he had a meal plan and pocket money.
>
> Not being prepared and planning ahead put me in a tough spot. I thought his dad would help. Then I realized I had to be the one to help. He worked so hard. I couldn't not help. It was $10,000. It was a lot. But I couldn't be the one to say no to his dream.
>
> But I also have two other children at home. I was playing chess with all my other responsibilities. I felt cornered. I took out an expensive online loan. No regular bank would give us a loan so it was the best we could do. I understand why, though. If you don't have the right credit score the banks can't help you. I wish the loan was cheaper, but it meant our son could go to college. Otherwise he probably would have had to delay going to school.

My son is doing great in school and he's already got a paid internship this summer! His success has made us better, too. I'm taking college courses so I can get a higher paying job and we're putting money away for my younger child and my grandchildren. I don't want them to have high-interest debt or student debt. I want them to have the habit of saving.

Parents like Lucy are increasingly faced with a terrible dilemma. Do they help out their kids, knowing that it will eat into already limited retirement savings or practice "tough love?" Tightropers have been through difficult financial situations and know just how hard it can be on young adults and young families. It can feel heartless for a Tightroper to not help in any way possible. But this often means taking on debt.

To help parents support their children's higher educational aspirations, the US government established the Parent PLUS program in 1965. Initially there were limits on the amount of borrowing, but these were lifted by Congress in 1993. The Parent PLUS program currently supports 3.4 million families. It's just one of the many types of debt that Tightropers take on to help their adult children.

As an example of the impact of student debt on Tightroper families, parents who borrow using Parent PLUS are now taking out an average of $16,400 per year in their own names to pay for tuition and other expenses. This is up dramatically from 1990, when it was only $5,200 per year (adjusted for inflation). And that's just for one child and one year. The average loan balances for parents who use the Parent PLUS program is now $25,600 and rising.[8] Shockingly, almost 10% of the parents using the program have accumulated over $100,000 of debt.

This leads to rising defaults for struggling Tightroper families: 11% of parents in the Parent PLUS program are in default. Unfortunately for them, the government is harder to deal with than private lenders. For PLUS loans in default, the government can garnish wages, take away Social Security benefits, or hold on to tax refunds.

And that isn't the end to the financial sacrifices that Tightroper parents make for their children. A survey by Creditcards.com found that 74% of parents paid at least some routine bills on behalf of their adult children. Cell phone expenses were the most common to be paid from the "Bank of Mom and Dad," followed by car payments and repairs. Based on the results of the study, they estimated that "49 million parents have yet to fully cut the financial umbilical cord from their grown-up offspring."[9]

In the previous section, I suggested that the college system is increasingly rigged against young Tightropers and their families and recommended that we rethink the value of a traditional college education in today's unstable and fast-paced society. I am not about to do the same for parenting. Obviously, we need to support parents and help them raise children without undue financial hardships.

I remain in awe of my sister raising four strong-willed children and humbled by the challenges my sister-in-law has faced having to fight the healthcare system to get proper medical treatments for her daughter. But why must they choose between the American Dream for themselves or their children? Can't we do better for Tightropers?

There are no easy answers to this problem. I remain extremely skeptical about the viability and ultimate effectiveness of massive governmental programs for addressing these issues. The cost of any programs to "solve" financial instability for upwards of half of the country are astronomical and the potential for unintended consequences is terrifying.

An easier place to focus our attention is the private sector. Not because corporate America can be counted on to sacrifice for the good of the country, but because innovators in this area stand to reap financial benefits.

Improving Workplace Flexibility

It's time for employers to be a part of the solution. The battle for talent is being fought more aggressively than ever before and an increasing number of employers offer special non-compensation benefits to attract and retain high-quality employees. Unfortunately, many of the employee perks seem to be designed for adolescent boys rather than responsible Tightropers:

- Almost every technology company has game rooms with ping pong and foosball tables.
- Salesforce offers gym memberships with massages, meditation, and a nutritionist on staff.

- *HuffPost* offers nap times for employees (some employers even have special "nap pods" to help minimize distractions!).
- VMware has "fur-ternity" leave for new pet owners as well as pet bereavement time.

While there is nothing wrong with these employee benefits, they are hardly making a difference in the long-term financial lives of employees. What Tightropers really need to support their families and help build savings are increased work flexibility and help with childcare.

Parenting isn't a nine-to-five job. From birth to when they leave the household (and in some cases beyond), children cause regular upheavals in the lives of their parents. Sickness, unexpected daycare needs, and important events that call for parental support all can make it a challenge to be at work, on time, every day. So why don't employers plan for these distractions and provide work environments with more flexibility?

The COVID-19 pandemic proved that work-at-home programs can be successful, but we need to make them an ongoing option for stressed parents.

As a CEO, I know this is easier said than done. Small teams and retail organizations simply can't manage effectively and deliver superior customer service when key individuals take time off unexpectedly. In my current "start-up mode," I have only a few employees in our call center. How do we handle call volume if people don't show up for work? However, more established companies can and should provide flexibility for employees. In an environment where companies vie aggressively for top talent, this can provide an important advantage.

A good place to start is with parental leave programs. Etsy, Netflix, and others are taking the lead by offering full maternity and paternity benefits as well as time off for adoption (which can be an even bigger adjustment for a young family than childbirth). Estée Lauder, as a further example, offers twenty weeks paid leave to parents regardless of sex, gender, or sexual orientation.

Oddly, the biggest obstacles to these types of benefits programs are the HR departments that should be championing them. In fact, when I implemented a very liberal maternity leave program (fourteen weeks) at a previous company, the fiercest resistance came from the head of HR. I had been pushing for the change because I was worried about two important employees who might leave the company in search of additional job flexibility as young mothers. The HR department, on the other hand, was worried about the potential for abuse (I'm still not sure I understand the issue!) and the distractions to her team from administering the program.

HR departments, like the rest of us, need to recognize that the world is changing rapidly and that they need to evolve to support the emerging financial realities facing Tightroper families.

Leading employers will learn how to adjust their workplace environments to the needs of Tightroper parents. This will pay off with increased loyalty from employees who value the flexibility and commitment of their employers. In fact, in a 2018 Zenefits study, 73% of employees said flexible work arrangements increased their satisfaction at work and 77% of employees listed flexible work as a primary consideration when evaluating future job opportunities.[10]

New Models for
Childcare in the Twenty-First Century

In the days of *Leave it to Beaver, The Brady Bunch,* and even *Everybody Loves Raymond,* childcare was filled with psychological challenges, but never fiscal ones. Dad had a career and Mom took care of the kids. The only problems were the hijinks the kids got into.

This was, of course, a TV fantasy that has been replaced by a very different reality. According to the Bureau of Labor Statistics, in over 60% of married families with children, both parents work. And that ignores the growth of single-parent households—35% of children are now raised by single parents.[11]

Childcare can no longer be taken for granted and it is one of the biggest pressures keeping parents on the Tightrope. Unfortunately, most current options for childcare aren't great. They're expensive and inflexible.

The Economic Policy Institute analyzed childcare costs across the United States and found that on average, infant care costs $786 per month and care for a four-year-old costs $625 per month.[12] That means that childcare for one infant can cost young Tightroper families almost 20% of their take-home pay, and the cost of one infant and one four-year-old can be more than the average monthly rent.

Some employers have stepped up to help Tightropers manage careers and families with less stress.

- Home Depot offers "back up dependent care" when employees need to be at work and regular childcare is unavailable. They make this available to employees up to ten days per year.
- Nike's World Headquarters in Beaverton, Oregon, houses a Child Development Team that provides childcare to hundreds of employees. They have committed to expand to other locations by partnering with third-party providers.
- Cisco offers childcare to children from six weeks to twelve years old on their larger campuses with accredited childcare providers. They also arrange for backup care in employee homes for unexpected events.

Some coworking facilities have also attempted to address this critical need by providing on-site childcare for members. This could be a compelling competitive advantage in the market for flexible, entrepreneurial office space. In fact, a coworking space network focused on women called **The Wing** found that "childcare was one of the top requested things from our network."[13]

One would like to believe that an "Uber for Childcare" could make a difference for struggling young Tightroper families, but so far the services provided tend to be for the affluent few rather than the mainstream. In the past few years, start-ups with names like **Zum**, **Shuddle**, and **HopSkip-Drive** have been founded to "provide children and parents with a trustworthy, professionally trained childcare and driving service and create peace of mind for the families" (according to a Zum press release). However, Zum charges a minimum of $16 for a ride and an eye-popping $6 per fifteen minutes of childcare.[14]

How can the government help with the challenges of affordable childcare for American families? In my mind, one of the easiest approaches would be tax incentives for employers to support childcare. This would drive adoption of these critical programs without requiring vast sums of government spending and administrative oversight.

As a society, we have given millions of parents a terrible choice—raise a family or retire comfortably. This is an unacceptable situation and change is desperately needed.

One of the few benefits of the COVID-19 pandemic is that it has taught us that work can be far more flexible and still be productive. Thanks to the lessons of this painful time, we can transform our society into one that is far more supportive of the unique pressures facing Tightroper families.

11

JOB INSTABILITY AND ENTREPRENEURSHIP

Retrenching, retooling, and taking risk

- Career setbacks can hit at any time but are devastating in midlife.
- Instability is turning everyone into entrepreneurs.
- Lifelong learning is a bridge between career changes but must be enhanced for better results.
- Financial apps can help support midlife Tightropers.
- Hardship protections are needed to cushion job transitions.

Your thirties and forties are when things can come together from a career perspective. You have enough experience and connections to feel comfortable and competent in your profession. Typically, you have had both successes and failures along the way; both shape your perspective and allow you to build the career you want.

The development of a career and the resulting financial stability used to be largely under your control. If you worked hard and did a good job, eventually your efforts would be noticed, and you would receive promotions and increased income. However, this is no longer the case. All of us now need to assume that any number of factors outside our control could eliminate or fundamentally restructure our jobs. This could be the impact of increased competition, new technology, globalization, changing consumer behaviors, or a global pandemic, but it leads to the same result—getting off the career ladder and having to retrench and restart in midlife to get back on track.

Barbara is currently a member of the gig economy after years of working for a large, established company.

> *I was let go when my company lost its biggest account and shut down unexpectedly. All the equity I had built up over the years was gone—just like that. Recently I've been driving for Uber, but my credit has taken a big hit. A couple of minor dings on my credit report and now I can't get the rates I need to buy a new car.*

Despite the many articles celebrating people who have moved on to new careers in midlife, the truth is far more sobering. According to a study by AARP, most people in midlife or later who become unemployed eventually accept a job with similar or lower pay,[1] like Barbara. And the longer you're unemployed, the more likely you are to accept a lower-paying job.

In the years leading up to the COVID-19 pandemic, the low unemployment rate was cold comfort for midlife workers like Barbara who lost their jobs because of business setbacks outside their control, changing market demands, or outdated technical skills. Although there were other jobs available, they often required new training (which can be expensive and time-consuming) and left people feeling like they were starting their career over. Now with the economic devastation of the COVID-19 pandemic, there may not be new jobs to train for.

The rule of thumb for finding a new job is that it can take a month for each $10,000 of expected income. This means that those looking for more than a $100,000 salary may wait a year or longer. This is part of the reason that the Tightroper phenomenon is not driven primarily by income level. Previously high earners can rapidly deplete their savings as they look for new employment, and they may be required to move to a new location for work, creating even more expense.

Rising job instability and the growth of gig work is turning the US into a country of entrepreneurs. Uber drivers, Instacart shoppers, and other self-employed Tightropers share a goal: to provide for themselves and their families in challenging and rapidly changing times.

Chanelle is an example of a Tightroper trying to take control of her finances.

After years as a hairstylist working for other people, she decided to open her own salon. She loves it, but it's been a challenge financially. Cosmetology school taught her how to cut and style hair—but not about cash flow and business ownership.

> *I've been cutting hair for about ten years and I was paying a lot of money to other barbershop owners—$200 per week to rent the chair, which is pricey. Once I learned the business, I decided to start out on my own.*
>
> *Honestly, I'm the type of person that once something is set in my head, I'm going to do it. It's gonna get done. Any sort of entrepreneurship you do is a risk—it's sink or swim—but I did my research.*
>
> *But nothing really prepares you for owning a business. Once you start a business it takes a toll on your credit. My cash flow is uneven—lumpy they call it. I had done a lot of work to build my credit but once I opened my business, it kind of slipped.*

Contrary to the popular image of the young start-up founder in skinny jeans and a hoodie, the average age of an entrepreneur starting his or her first business is forty years old.[2] With ten to twenty years of work experience, people often wonder if they could make more money and be more satisfied working for themselves.

However, as a serial entrepreneur who once sold my house to fund a new business idea, I can vouch for the fact that it is incredibly risky and prone to failure. Some articles have claimed that as many as 90% of start-ups are doomed to fail. Fortunately, that number is overstated, but according to the Small Business Administration, at best only 50% of start-ups will survive more than five years.

It takes money to start a business, and midlife entrepreneurship can conflict with other cherished financial priorities: putting children through college, paying off the house, saving for retirement, and perhaps investing in a vacation home or rental property. And many midlife Tightropers don't have much of a cash cushion for their households, never mind one that could insulate their households from the cash drain of a start-up.

Entrepreneurial Tightropers believe in themselves more than the start-up gurus do. To make her dream come to life, Chanelle used family help and small business loans, as well as personal loans. She's making it, but there's not much left over right now.

Lifelong Learning for a Lifetime of Job Changes

Midlife Tightropers get it. In most cases, the job and career they planned on didn't happen or evolved into something they didn't expect. And career disruption can happen in any field, at any time.

They don't want handouts, they want a helping hand. They need tools to help them respond to these changes—starting with ongoing job retraining programs. However, taking years to learn a new field isn't realistic. Tightropers managing families on tight budgets need educational alternatives that are affordable and align with their multi-threaded lifestyles.

Once again, the for-profit education sector has taken the lead on retraining midlife Tightropers. Of course, there have been widely publicized abuses, such as the so-called culinary schools that put students in debt for tens of thousands of dollars and delivered very low-paying jobs (if any). However, more responsible for-profit colleges are trying to provide new types of training and certification programs that are better suited to midlife Tightropers than traditional college programs.

Technology-based instruction has the potential to provide far more targeted education and training at a fraction of the cost of traditional colleges. Given the phenomenal success of online courses such as foreign language instruction, is there a need for classroom instruction for most curricula? Certainly the shelter-in-place orders caused by COVID-19 have forced the country to test just how far we can go with nontraditional education.

Unfortunately, online training and certification programs are rarely realistic enough to substitute for actual on-the-job experience and can be extremely expensive—often as costly as on-campus programs. There is no reason we should accept either of these situations. More sophisticated A.I.-based training programs can do a far better job of simulating on-the-job challenges—even teamwork activities. And improved technology should yield lower-cost solutions.

Kathy Boden Holland, the President of Adtalem Global Education's Medical and Healthcare Group, a for-profit education company primarily focused on healthcare, has no choice but to fully commit to online programs. "Two-thirds of our students are actually online," says Kathy. "They are typically people who are fueled by a desire to achieve and caffeine but must balance classwork, part-time jobs, and family—all across the country." However, Kathy believes that at present, purely online programs are insufficient for certain professional careers like healthcare.

"The key is to deliver a full experience for our students that helps them simulate what they will face in real clinical situations." Kathy said that they are looking to partner with hospitals to create hybrid programs that combine the online training with real-world "practicums." This is all to forward their goal of making students more "practice-ready" when they graduate.

This is not just a challenge for companies like Adtalem, which trains doctors, veterinarians, and nurses. Almost all jobs require people to work effectively in teams and to clearly communicate and persuade coworkers, supervisors, and customers. These skills need to be a critical component of all college coursework and training programs—potentially in close coordination with employers.

Recently, the US Treasury called for mandatory financial literacy courses for college students. It is unclear to me whether financial literacy programs provide real value to Tightropers. More critical and more beneficial to Tightropers, in my opinion, would be mandatory business management training in high school. As we've seen, an increasing number of Tightropers graduate directly from high school or college into a life of gig work and entrepreneurship. With basic levels of instruction, millions of Tightropers could be ready to hit the ground running in the workforce, rather than being forced to learn essential financial skills while finding their way for the first time in the business world.

Financial Apps That Work For Tightropers

The long-term effect of the rise of the Side Hustle in the US is that fewer and fewer Tightropers will rely on the mythical "lifetime" employment. Instead, they will need to be entrepreneurial to find and manage jobs and income streams throughout their lives.

Historically, our financial system was great for wealthy individuals and established companies, but ignored the needs of Tightropers and the self-employed. Fortunately, Silicon Valley technology innovators are starting to develop tools to support the changing financial and career needs of Tightropers.

Numerous "challenger banks" such as **Chime**, **Dave**, and **Varo** have attracted millions of new account holders—many of them Tightropers—by providing "early paydays" for consumers (that is, making direct deposit income available up to two days earlier than traditional banks). Going even further, some challenger banks have been designed from the ground up for the unique needs of self-employed Tightropers.

Azlo is one of several examples of how business banking is being reinvented for time-constrained, entrepreneurial Tightropers. Azlo is a no-fee bank that helps customers make payments (to vendors, employees, and themselves) and manage and track invoices. It's easy to use and doesn't assume that customers have a degree in accounting. The business model is compelling precisely because they aren't trying to be everything to everyone. They don't take cash deposits and don't offer checkbooks. And unlike most big banks, they provide webinars and training on topics of interest to entrepreneurs.

Oxygen Bank also adds in "cash-flow" based credit to support the variable cash flows of gig workers and entrepreneurs. Like Azlo, they don't charge monthly fees and provide one-time "virtual" cards that let customers manage payments without having to provide their banking or credit card details.

Better banking solutions are just one piece of the puzzle. As we learned from Antonio and Kelly's moving story, managing your finances without having an employer withhold for taxes can lead to big cashflow problems. Instead of requiring complicated tax forms and forcing people to make difficult decisions about tax, social security, and other withholdings, Tightropers need new "set it and forget it" software apps that integrate with their bank accounts and ensure that Tightropers are putting money into savings and properly dealing with taxes and other requirements.

A company called **Track.Tax** is working to take the pain and unexpected surprises out of tax withholding for self-employed Tightropers. They use machine-learning to track expected federal and state taxes on self-employment (1099) income, including FICA, Medicare, and federal income taxes, using income and expense information imported directly from your bank account. Based on this information, they can withhold taxes into FDIC-insured accounts, make quarterly tax payments, and process tax documents.

Another important new type of financial app puts economic bargaining power in the hands of consumers and helps them negotiate lower priced services with less hassle and risk.

Truebill helps customers detect unwanted subscriptions and negotiate lower monthly bills. They say that their app "magically" gives you a complete picture of your finances. What that means is they connect with customers' credit card and bank account transaction data to identify recurring bills and improper charges. Users can cancel unwanted recurring bills with a click and Truebill will split any cost savings they negotiate 60/40 with customers (they take 40% of the annual savings).

They also continue to monitor customer spending on a daily basis to identify unusual expenses that may be fraudulent or increases in charges from existing billers. Interestingly, they also monitor outages on cable and internet service providers across the country. If there's a temporary outage on your cable or internet service, Truebill can request a credit to your account.

Billshark is another digital money assistant app that negotiates with a wide variety of billers including cable, cell phone, satellite TV, and even home security systems to lower rates for customers. Like Truebill, they take 40% of the savings they deliver to their customers.

Trim provides many of the same benefits as Billshark and Truebill. It can cancel unwanted recurring expenses and negotiate lower bills. Trim claims they can reduce any cable, internet, or phone bill by up to 30% and they take 33% of the annualized savings. It also tries to help customers increase their savings with a product called Trim Simple Savings that tracks and analyzes bank and credit card transactions to come up with specific recommendations for users.

Clarity Money is somewhat more "holistic" than other financial apps. In addition to negotiating bills and canceling unwanted subscriptions (for 33% of the annual savings), Clarity Money supports a broad range of linked accounts including retirement accounts. They even offer free credit-score monitoring.

Not to be outdone, **Harvest** uses machine-learning to identify fees that are likely to be refunded and contacts the billers directly on behalf of their customers. They are the low-price leader in this space at present by charging "only" 25% of the savings.

One can easily see where this is leading, and it should be great news for Tightropers. The cost to consumers of these services will continue to drop with competition and the insights into cost savings will become deeper and more beneficial. Innovative apps like these will become increasingly integrated into the financial lives of Tightropers and serve as robo-advisors constantly looking out for their economic interests.

Give Tightropers a Break

Improved lifetime learning and innovative financial apps are great—but when you lose your job, they aren't an immediate fix. Midlife dislocations happen suddenly, but the financial impacts linger and can cause a downward spiral if exacerbated by aggressive lenders and landlords.

Tightropers are willing to reskill for new opportunities, but that takes time and time is money. Tightropers need a financial break while they are retooling for the next career opportunity. The government can help by providing additional tax breaks for people training for new work opportunities as well as by passing key legislation to provide an expanded safety net for job loss. This should include improved unemployment benefits, healthcare during unemployment, rent support, and credit forbearance.

Many responsible companies currently work with their customers to help them manage between income streams because they know it's the best way to ultimately get paid and maintain a customer relationship. **Lending Club** offers "hardship plans" for borrowers experiencing job loss or other unexpected life events. Under the plan, borrowers are allowed to temporarily make interest-only payments for a period of three months to accommodate an unexpected life event. After three months, regular payment terms and obligations resume. My former company, **Elevate**, as well as many other nonprime lenders, offered similarly flexible hardship plans for customers impacted by the COVID-19 pandemic.

Large property managers have told me the same thing. It is far more costly for them to evict a renter than to be flexible while they manage through job loss or other unexpected financial setbacks. Building flexibility into products and services for the types of real-world upheavals that Tightropers face allows leading companies to maintain longer and more profitable lifetime customer relationships.

This is where government can help. Not all companies are as ethical and understanding about the financial hardships of their customers. The days of baseball bat-wielding collectors are fortunately long gone, but aggressive practices remain and some even take customers to court if they miss loan payments.

Now that nearly half of Americans struggle with financial insecurity, it is time to rewrite the playbook to give them a break while they are in between jobs and preparing for the next one.

12

MIDLIFE DEBT TRAPS

When debt stops helping and starts hurting

- Credit is essential for Tightropers—but can be dangerous.
- Americans are facing record levels of debt, and it's getting worse.
- We need improved protections and more responsible credit options designed specifically for Tightropers.

F amily issues can become financial issues, and Tightropers often reach for credit to survive. But for Diane and Sara, this quickly got out of control.

I'm embarrassed to be in this situation, but I don't know what I could have done.

Our child was diagnosed with autism and needed more of my time so I had to cut back on work. Then I got a hernia and, since work required me to stand, I had to take time off to focus on getting healthy and taking care of my son.

I needed credit. I first started with credit cards—I call them Vulture Cards—and then had to borrow even more. I got payday loans and high-interest online loans. They helped me get by, but I knew I had to do something about all of the debt I had accumulated.

It's not like we were careless, but it took us longer than it should have to get things back under control. I sold stuff on eBay, downsized as much as possible—even doubled the size of my car insurance deductible to get costs down. We still have a ton of debt, but it's getting better.

Credit is an important part of a well-functioning economy. It helps people afford large purchases like homes and cars and is essential for most to start and grow small businesses.

For Tightropers like Diane and Sara, however, there is a point where debt becomes unmanageable. Too often, midlife challenges like family expenses, job changes, entrepreneurship, or health problems can cause debt to spiral out of control.

We've all read the articles about skyrocketing debt, but the growth in debt in this country is truly stunning. Driven by mortgages and student loans, overall consumer debt has approximately doubled every decade since the 1970s and is now over $4 trillion.

CHART 12.1. Growth in US Debt[1]

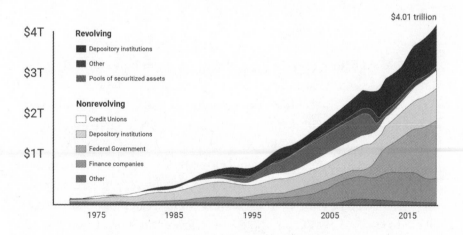

The majority of Americans (53%) cite debt reduction as their number one financial priority. High debt limits the ability of Tightropers to save and weather additional financial stress. In fact, 20% of Americans spend over half of their monthly income on debt repayment, making it nearly impossible for them to dig out from this burden.[2]

Credit card usage has skyrocketed since being introduced in the 1970s and can quickly get out of hand for Tightropers like Diane and Sara because it is so easy to get and so easy to rely on. For many Tightropers, credit cards become a case of "boiling the frog"—you don't know how bad the situation is until you're cooked. Shockingly, Tightropers (those with no or low savings) often have the highest credit card balances—over $10,000.

CHART 12.2. Average Credit Card Debt by Household Net Worth[3]

Household Net Worth

Credit card debt is also dangerous because it can be so difficult to escape. Because credit cards are "open-end" credit (unlike your mortgage or car loan which are "closed-end" installment loans), there is no fixed repayment term. Credit cards typically only require a small amount of active balances repaid each month, so even if you don't make any more purchases on the card, it can take an extremely long time to pay them off.

For instance, let's take a household with $10,000 in credit card debt. In this case, it can take more than twelve years of minimum payments to pay the credit card off in full and would result in over $6,500 in interest. And of course, it takes remarkable financial self-control to avoid using the card during the twelve-plus year repayment period.

Even worse, as the credit card gets paid off, the lack of utilization of the card will negatively impact the customer's credit score, making it hard to get low APR credit in the future. It can become a "doom loop" and a source of unending stress for Tightropers.

So what's the answer? Tightropers rely on credit to make it through unexpected events but for the same reason, too much reliance on credit can lead to negative outcomes.

Credit Innovation for Tightroper Realities

Tightropers need credit like oxygen to help maneuver through life's ups and downs. Without savings, unexpected bills and untimely job loss can quickly push people off their financial tightrope. Credit is what bridges the gap between expenses and income and helps people get back on stable ground.

Ron Suber has been called the "Godfather of Fintech" for good reason. He was the president of Prosper, a leading marketplace (or "peer-to-peer") lender, and has been a tireless promoter of (and investor in) financial technology innovators. His perspectives on ways to leverage technology to better serve people globally are instructive.

"Using technology—especially mobile technology—to provide financial inclusion to people is what's exciting to me," says Ron. "People deserve instant access to borrow, save or lend money—and in some ways the US is behind the rest of the world."

He correctly points out the flaws in traditional credit products like credit cards. "Credit cards are a great way to get frequent flyer points, but a terrible way to borrow money for cash-constrained people."

Ron highlights the fact that credit cards can lead to a lifelong cycle of debt. It is all too easy for Tightropers to ignore the impact of all the small purchases, and all too easy to only pay a small amount of the principal every month. This adds up quickly. In many ways, credit cards are specifically structured to lull customers into a false sense of security until—in many cases—it's too late.

What leading Fintech innovators do successfully, according to Ron, is to "start doing things that customers love," like no overdraft fees or monthly fees in the case of Chime and the other leading challenger banks.

Think about what Netflix did to Blockbuster as a great example of how disruptive it can be to eliminate customer pain points (e.g., late fees).

He sees a similar opportunity for serving Tightropers because of the unique financial stresses they face. "Their income hasn't kept up with their expenses and the Big Banks haven't really focused on their real issues by helping them smooth out their finances. They don't provide access to flexible credit and they pounce on the misfortunes of their customers with overdraft fees and returned payment fees," says Ron.

"Let's say Jo is in construction and she is an independent contractor. Jo has bills that are due, but she doesn't get paid until the end of the month. If she goes to her bank to borrow $500 or $1,000 based on an invoice that is due to be paid in two weeks, she'll be laughed out of the office. But there are a growing number of Fintechs who are eager to lend based on that invoice. And in many cases, there are no fees and no points upfront."

The problem for banks, says Ron, is that new financial technology innovators may "capture the hearts and minds of middle-income Americans" the way companies like Zillow and Redfin have taken over the real estate business. Although the potential is there, Ron agrees that there isn't a "killer app" yet for Fintech lending to Tightropers. Most of the initial innovative Fintech offerings have been focused on the needs of prime and superprime consumers.

What would a "killer app" for Tightropers look like? We can guess that it would be designed based on their unique financial needs and leverage technology to serve those needs better than legacy institutions like big banks. In particular, Tightropers will need products that fulfill the following requirements:

24-7 Convenience

It is remarkable that so many people in the world of consumer finance (especially nonprime consumer finance) continue to believe that customers prefer face to face interactions. Tightropers are like every other segment of society—they don't have time to drive and stand in line to be served. That's why online lending has taken off, even though it is often more expensive than brick and mortar alternatives.

However, simply providing online access is no longer a differentiator. Innovators need to step up with credit products that fund instantly into the customer's bank account—rather than overnight—and with mobile apps that provide financial data and insights that are accurate up to the minute.

No FICO Underwriting

As we've discussed throughout this book, FICO scores work for prime consumers but are far less valuable when underwriting Tightropers. FICO overstates the creditworthiness of customers struggling with recent cash flow problems and understates the ability to repay for consumers that have fully recovered from previous job loss or financial setbacks.

Fortunately, there is a solution. Many financial apps are now gaining real-time access to consumer bank accounts to provide much more accurate insights into the ability of the customer to afford a loan. Regulatory hurdles remain for using this data, but the potential upside for providing affordable (and profitable) credit to underserved Americans is tremendous.

Safety Net Credit

Because of their limited savings and high income volatility, Tightropers are more likely to struggle making on-time debt payments. Currently, most lenders deal with this with sky-high APRs, punitive fees, or aggressive collection practices or requirements to pledge personal collateral, like a car, in case of default.

But these can have harsh downsides for Tightropers. "Gotcha" pricing and punitive fees can make on-time repayment increasingly unrealistic. And even if the lender doesn't repossess your car (which is the outcome of 20% of all title loan transactions), reporting defaults to the credit bureaus makes it harder and harder to make it back to mainstream credit rates.

What Tightropers need is a "safety net" for their credit usage that provides limited financial pitfalls and more flexibility built-in for managing repayment uncertainty.

Safety Net Credit products for Tightropers may not be the lowest cost, but will be more supportive of their changing financial conditions. They will allow customers to easily restructure debt payments during times of financial hardship without negatively impacting the customer's credit score and will never rely on aggressive collections practices.

Innovative upstarts are beginning to integrate many of these features. Now it's time to see what works best and help Tightropers get to solid ground. As Ron Suber passionately states, "this is what Fintech should be all about—democratizing credit and helping people."

SECTION 4

Tightropers Facing Retirement

13

LAST CHANCE TO PREPARE FOR RETIREMENT

Millions of Americans won't be able to retire without help

- Aging is particularly terrifying for Tightropers who don't have the financial resources to retire comfortably.
- Tightropers continue to be self-reliant as they age, but they can only work for so long.
- Only by deeply understanding the unique pressures facing aging Tightropers can we design policies and products that can make a difference.

Deborah is a black belt. Not in karate, but at a refinery. It's a certification that allows her to help optimize the plant's work processes, lower costs, and improve safety. She lives in El Segundo, California, and has been in manufacturing for over thirty-seven years. Manufacturing has always been rewarding to Deborah because of the people, the diversity, and the challenge of being pushed "out of my comfort zone."

After her divorce, she made sure that her two children graduated high school in the best school district even though it was a more expensive part of town. She planned to move to a lower-cost neighborhood once her kids went off to college. But Deborah soon found out that it's not that easy to move away from the people who you care about.

A neighbor who was one of my best friends came down with cancer. We'd known each other for twenty-four years and even owned property together. I was planning to move away but I just couldn't leave.

I actually helped take care of her every night. It was the toughest time I've ever been through in my life—I was constantly exhausted. I had faith and just kept moving on and trying to do what I needed to do, which was to go to work every day, take care of my two kids, and take care of my friend.

I'm proud that we were able to take care of her without bringing anyone else in, which was what she wanted, until the last twenty-four hours of her life, when we brought in hospice.

When she eventually passed, her family got involved and it took about five months longer to sell the property than it should have. It was a scary time because the fact that we co-owned the property made everything so complicated. My credit took a dump after that. I ran up every credit card I had.

The stress was terrible. I was juggling so many bills, but I couldn't tell anyone about it because it's kind of embarrassing to tell people about your finances.

When the house finally sold it was such a relief. It's still very bittersweet because I lost a dear friend in the process along with the property we lived in for twenty-four years. But I was able to get out of the debt I had incurred.

The biggest financial fear of all is outliving your money.

Time and again, surveys by financial advisory groups and retirement planning think tanks highlight that vast numbers of aging Americans are haunted by this fear as they pass the midlife marker. They realize they have only a few more years to work and likely two or three decades to live on what they've accumulated...or not.

Everything around retirement planning is grounded in the assumption that people have stable income and can control their expenses to consistently put money away. The professionals put together rosy charts that show how much money you can expect to live on after retirement based on your monthly savings plans.

And all that works for the Safely Stable. They have managed to avoid the financial stresses and strains that keep their Tightroper neighbors in a life of limited resources. The Safely Stable are rightly proud of the financial discipline they have shown in their lives, the career success, and the appreciation of their investments including their homes.

Tightropers, however, often suffer a sense of shame when they struggle with limited retirement savings in late midlife. They look back and wonder—where did it all go? Why don't I have more put away?

Most Tightropers I've heard from in this situation don't make excuses. They recognize that there were things they could have done differently, vacations they could have skipped, financial decisions they wish had turned out better. And they are determined to use their remaining time before retirement to build as much of a cushion as possible.

Yet, still they give to the ones around them. They provide for adult children, their communities, and their own parents who may be struggling with health problems. They sacrifice selflessly for loved ones, fully aware of their own impending financial challenges.

Tightropers are fighters. They face life's setbacks with confidence and resilience. But for many Tightropers, the numbers just don't add up. About 45% of pre-retirees think they'll face the dreaded specter of outliving their savings, but simultaneously admit that they haven't done anything to address this concern.[1]

In typical Tightroper fashion, they're trying to figure out a "hack." Nearly half of pre-retirees think that working longer is the solution. That's how many expect to keep working past age sixty-five, and 18% of those same people expect to work until their early seventies.[2]

That is Anne's reality.

Escaping a dysfunctional workplace and escalating cost of living, she relocated from Los Angeles to the Coachella Valley in California for a life reset.

Like many Americans, she found her retirement cushion too thin to support her. Though she'd worked all her life, helping family members in crisis had drained her savings. Options seemed scarce, so she created some.

She bartered property management for a reduction in rent on an apartment. And she has become an expert at finding and landing short-term work. From delivering lunch and dinner to office-bound workers to helping out at events, Anne figured out how to derive satisfaction from her late-life gig work.

This isn't what I expected for my retirement. But I love the climate. I love to take walks and go to the pool. The biggest joy in my life is being able to do things on my own schedule. I was in the grind for forty years. Now I can be outside, putter around my garden and spend time with neighbors while I'm working. Even when I'm doing something as mundane as taking out the trash cans, I'm looking at the sky and the mountains, enjoying the simple pleasures.

Expecting to work until you die isn't a great answer for Tightropers. Our bodies won't physically hold up and the needs of those around us are likely to erode our income-earning potential. We need better and more constructive solutions for later-life Tightropers.

14

CARING FOR OTHERS—
NO GOOD DEED GOES UNPUNISHED

Caregiving erodes wealth and jeopardizes a stable retirement

- Precisely because they have more financial resources, Tightropers in their fifties and sixties are often called upon to support adult children and aging parents.
- Commitment to their loved ones in the form of care for adult children, eldercare, and spousal healthcare can quickly wipe out savings, resulting in Tightropers entering their retirement years with little to live on.
- As a society, we should reward aging caregivers and help them build for retirement.

Caryn works with judges at the Texas Supreme Court. She loves being around such smart, capable people. It keeps her on her toes! However, the pay isn't great, and it's been hard to put money aside because of all the people who are counting on her.

My father had a stroke in '99 and lost his income. And after he died, my mom's been on a very limited fixed income ever since. She was always a strong woman but lately she's been declining, and I've had to help out more and more. I'm glad she's still independent, it would be a lot harder if I had to put her in a facility.

I give her money every month, but she comes short pretty often. This month it was the water bill that I had to cover. And on top of that, I had to help pay the insurance for my niece.

My mom's funny—she never openly asks for money. But I can tell when things are tight because she'll stay in her house and refuse to do things. Recently she wasn't going to go to a birthday party because she didn't have money to buy a present! That's crazy.

I've had to sacrifice for myself, though. I had some procedures that should have been done but I keep postponing them until I can put some money away. My oncologist actually "dropped" me because I didn't have the money to get the biopsy she'd ordered.

I have a twin—for better or worse. She used to be a drain on the family and since our names and social security numbers are so close, she was always messing up my credit score. Things are better now that she's living with me. She doesn't help with the house but she's trying to get her life together. But it's one more person in the family I've got to take care of.

It's a lot of responsibility but I'm proud that I'm keeping it all together. Even if sometimes I have to eat a lot of peanut butter sandwiches to make it work.

As we age, we understand the need to plan for retirement. However, there's one factor that annihilates our well-made plans, including the Safely Stable: when the people you love need help, you help them out.

You help if a parent shows signs of early Alzheimer's or dementia. You help if your adult daughter struggles with the financial and emotional stress of a painful divorce. And you do whatever it takes to get by when your household income gets cut and medical expenses surge due to the health problems of a spouse.

This may mean taking a second (or third) job or having to cut back paid work hours to be a caregiver. Tightropers in this situation often run up credit cards, tap home equity, or take out high-interest loans. Consistently, you will hear from them that "family comes first."

Caregiving and close relationships are profound factors in the lives of all Tightropers, but especially those in late midlife and into retirement. In their circles, they are the ones who have something to borrow against because, despite all odds, they've managed to accumulate some home equity, hold on to jobs, and build some savings. They are often better off than younger and older loved ones, who, respectively, have not yet saved or have eaten through their savings.

Pulled from both generational directions, Tightropers in late midlife and into retirement understand the consequences of hollowing out their meager assets to help others...and still they help. And as a society, we should help them.

Caring for Elders

It's easy to understand the "math of the moment" that propels Baby Boomer Tightropers like Caryn to give up their hopes for retirement to care for their aging relatives. As of this writing, the average annual cost of a bed in a semiprivate room in a nursing home is $85,775. That number is 3.7 times the average annual income of Americans over age sixty-five (which is only $23,394).[1]

Tightroper families can't afford that. End-of-life care in America wipes out a lifetime of work, saving, and financial responsibility in just a few years. No wonder families stave off institutional care as long as possible, even if it means they shoulder the heart-wrenching caregiving responsibilities themselves.

Eldercare responsibilities peak in late midlife—especially for people in their fifties and sixties. More than 10% of Americans between fifty and sixty-five are currently taking care of ailing relatives.[2] This is a terrible financial setback at precisely the time when Tightropers may have finally set aside enough money to think about a less precarious financial existence. Instead, eldercare responsibilities keep them on the Tightrope right up until retirement.

Paying to support aging loved ones is a challenge for Tightroper families, but in some ways, the time and energy spent on elderly parents is even more draining—physically, emotionally, and financially.

83% of care to older adults with long-term needs is provided by friends or family members. But that isn't really free. Caregivers often have to cut back on their hours at work and may find their own health impacted. In fact, 70% of caregivers suffer work-related difficulties due to their caregiving duties.[3]

The rise of dementia and Alzheimer's cases in the US is particularly difficult for Tightropers who want to take care of their declining parent.

It costs an estimated $341,840 on average to take care of a parent with dementia or Alzheimer's for the rest of his/her life.[4] This is a massive financial drain. That's why so many Tightropers in their late midlife move their parents back home.

I can speak to the selflessness required in these situations having watched my father provide daily loving support to his wife with Alzheimer's and more recently my sister-in-law bravely care for my brother when he was diagnosed with very early-onset Alzheimer's.

The problem of eldercare for millions of Americans coming up on retirement is strangely ignored in the press and by politicians. It doesn't fit any of the left vs. right narratives. On one hand, it's a failure of our healthcare system that families need to take care of their own despite the horrific impact on their financial well-being. On the other hand, it's a triumph of individual responsibility and sacrifice for the good of our loved ones. It should be something that we can all rally around—but the silence is deafening.

In a compelling article in the *Washington Monthly*, Grace Gedye interviewed Howard Gleckman, a Senior Fellow at the Urban-Brookings Tax Policy Center about the issue. He said that when talking to members of Congress about eldercare, "you can divide the world of politicians into two groups. It's not Democrats and Republicans, it's people who have been caregivers and people who haven't."[5] For an issue that is so critical to our societal health, we need to increase visibility and focus on improved support and solutions—in particular for Tightroper families who are hollowing out their already limited retirement savings to support their families.

Caring for Themselves

Now in her late fifties, Sandy has lived in southeastern Ohio for nearly her entire life. For decades, she worked as a pharmaceutical technician while her husband worked—time and a half—as a police officer. Then a cascade of medical events sidelined him into permanent disability and threw their financial stability into chaos.

> We were a two-income family making $80,000 a year then all of a sudden we became a one-income family only making $40,000.

I was supporting my husband full time and of course helping my daughter on occasion as well. My main goal was not to lose our house, but it was a constant challenge. The medical bills just kept coming and even though I've got insurance, copayments were sometimes thousands of dollars.

Sometimes it felt like I was working two full-time jobs. I had my day job like before, but I also had to deal with my husband's medical situation. He had trouble with getting around, and of course I had to do all the housework.

Our credit took a huge hit. We fell behind on credit card bills, had trouble making car payments, and took out expense loans. Before long, our credit score was only 400. I didn't even think that was possible!

We couldn't get a new car and couldn't get anyone to lend us money for new carpeting or to repair the roof. A lot of times, we just went without. It took us five years to pay everything off. By then, your credit is ruined. And once your credit is ruined, nobody cares about you.

We kept at it, though. We managed to get our credit score back up to almost 660 and we were able to buy a truck.

I was homeless as a kid. My father was sick, and I had eight siblings, and the next thing you know, you're living with aunts and uncles. It was bad. Keeping a roof over my head was the most important thing. Being homeless—that's never going to happen to me again.

With her husband entering the traditional retirement age with compromised health and with their savings depleted, Sandy knows that she'll have to continue working, in some capacity, past age sixty-five to rebuild.

It's worth it, she said, to build a financial firewall between her family and the too-real threat of losing everything and being unable to recover.

The stories that Tightropers tell about the decisions they make to take care of adult children or aging parents are filled with a combination of pain and pride. They are fully aware of the financial challenges they are taking on but happy to be able to help out family members and friends in need.

This is not the case when an older Tightroper or their spouse deals with their own serious healthcare issues. When this happens, there is only pain and sacrifice. Whether the primary breadwinner has to cut back on their work hours or quit work entirely, health issues for aging Americans are devastating to their income and sense of financial independence.

And, of course, healthcare in this country isn't free. As Sandy highlighted, even people with good insurance coverage face high deductibles and copay expenses.

As a very minor example, my wife suffered from some hip pain. A lifelong tennis player and yoga enthusiast, this was keeping her from engaging in her favorite activities. When she went to the doctor to get an MRI, they charged her $1,600 out of pocket, which was approved by our insurance provider. However, several weeks later we received a bill for another $1,000! We were fortunate to have the financial resources for this unexpected expense, but that would have been a massive setback to savings for Tightropers in our age group.

Michelle is another Tightroper facing hardship due to health problems. She got sick but was confident since her husband had excellent insurance through his employer.

> I couldn't walk and I couldn't get up and down stairs. Our home is on the second floor with eleven steps. On top of that it's got a sunken living room kind of thing. Seemed great when we bought the house but not so good in a wheelchair.
>
> I knew we'd have medical expenses but there was so much more cost! We had to buy ramps and install one of those stair lifts. They aren't cheap—ramps alone are $500. And when my husband was at work, we had to pay out of pocket for someone to come and help me around. Even with our insurance my health problems basically wiped us out.
>
> I'm really ticked off about our healthcare system. We had a Democratic house, a Democratic senate, and a Democratic president and we still couldn't get universal coverage. Obamacare was just like this piecemeal thing.

Michelle is right to be frustrated with healthcare in this country. In 2000, long-term care expenditures in the US totaled $30 billion annually. As of 2015, that number jumped to $225 billion.[6] That's an increase of 650%! This can't continue—we need to reduce the financial impact on aging Americans and their families.

Caregiving:
Honorable Sacrifice or Financial Pitfall?

The numbers are staggering:

- 34.2 million: The number of Americans who have provided unpaid care to an adult fifty or over in the past twelve months.
- 16.1 million: The number of caregivers for someone with Alzheimer's or dementia.
- $470 billion: The estimated dollar value of long-term care provided by unpaid caregivers (2013).[7]

It's hard to say no. Not when the choice is investing in your children's future or expressing faithfulness and loyalty for a lifetime of care extended to you by your own parents. Yet, the culture of caregiving—while laudable, humane, and wholly logical in its own context—frays the tightrope.

When Tightropers suspend paid work to tend to children or aging parents full time, they forfeit more than a few promotions and professional growth. They also stunt their eventual Social Security payout and their lifetime earnings. Because you can't save what you haven't earned, truncated or fragmented career paths lead to lower savings and investments, impacting immediate financial security and long-term sustenance.

This sacrifice falls mainly on women, who represent two-thirds of all caregivers. Women are expected to step up first for caregiving. Generally, daughters (starting with the eldest) and then daughters-in-law are expected to pitch in before any adult son is expected to help with daily caregiving. They are also taking a terrible financial hardship. A woman over age fifty who quits her job to pick up caregiving will forfeit a crippling total of $324,044 in earnings and entitlements.[8]

If humans were purely economic beings, they would ignore the needs of loved ones and focus their efforts exclusively on building for a stable and well-funded retirement. Thankfully, most of us make supporting our families and communities a critical priority in our lives—even to the detriment of our own financial well-being. It's our greatest human trait and what makes society work.

The sacrifices made every day by hardworking Tightropers for their families and loved ones should be supported and rewarded, but in many ways our public policies work against them. For instance, the tax code allows people to write off out-of-pocket expenses (ramps, nursing homes, drugs), but for some reason we penalize the people who want to take care of their loved ones themselves. Out-of-pocket long-term care costs represent less than 20% of overall costs paid by families.[9] Do we really want to provide incentives to push people away from families and into already overstretched and often impersonal care facilities? Not to mention the danger of contagion that is endemic to nursing homes.

Another example of how current policies don't support aging Tightropers is the earned-income tax credit. For a family with two qualifying children, the EITC can provide nearly $6,000 annually and is used by millions of younger Tightropers as an important benefit to help get by and build savings. However, the EITC is only a benefit for those with job income. It isn't available for unpaid caregivers and in any event doesn't provide for families that have dependent adult children unless they are "permanently and totally disabled."

This disconnect between how we want people to act—caring and supportive—and how we penalize people when they make economic sacrifices for others is a tragedy. Hard-heartedness should not be the solution to the midlife and retirement collision of caregiving and financial instability impacting so many Tightropers.

In previous chapters, I've focused on the things that private sector innovation can do to make a difference in the lives of Tightropers. For good reason: in our current polarized and gridlocked political environment, it's hard to bet on politicians delivering the kind of legislation and spending programs that will make a difference. The best and fastest solutions come when innovators spring into action to address a new market opportunity.

However, for older Tightropers, the issues are quite different. The numbers are simply too big and existing private solutions have largely failed.

In order to better understand the policy options for addressing the needs of aging Tightroper caregivers, I spoke with Howard Gleckman at the Urban-Brookings Tax Policy Center. In addition to being an influential nonpartisan scholar on tax issues, he wrote a moving book on the challenges of eldercare in this country, called *Caring for Our Parents: Inspiring Stories of Families Seeking New Solutions to America's Most Urgent Health Crisis.*[10]

What immediately became clear from talking with Howard is that the options for eldercare are getting worse. Traditional nursing homes are shutting down because they don't make enough money from Medicaid and Medicare payments. In fact, 4% of nursing homes—both for-profit and nonprofit—closed between 2015 and 2019. And this trend is accelerating because it simply doesn't make economic sense any longer.

Furthermore, Howard points to the shortage of in-home care workers as a serious problem. "I have never in my life seen this before, but home care agencies are now requiring aides making $10 an hour to sign non-compete agreements. The labor shortages in the market are causing companies to go to that extreme. It is a very difficult job with very high injury rates, yet we still underpay workers and they usually don't receive any benefits. To put things in perspective, we pay veterinary technicians more than home care workers—that tells me that we care more for our cats than our loved ones."

The insurance industry has also largely given up on long-term care. According to Howard, "when I wrote the book ten years ago, insurance providers were selling 750,000 standalone policies a year (which wasn't nearly enough). Last year, according to the most recent industry data, they sold a mere 60,000 policies." That's more than a 90% reduction in the volume of long-term care insurance policies from just a decade ago.

Howard calls the situation a "Harvard Business School case study on market failure—consumers don't want to buy it and carriers don't want to sell it." In many ways, this situation has been fueled by the growth of Tightropers in this country. With limited savings, it's hard to justify investing in long-term insurance—more immediate financial needs take precedence.

This situation is gaining awareness in Washington, DC. In fact, former Democratic presidential candidate Pete Buttigieg's team reached out to Howard to try to come up with policy solutions during his run for President. Howard said it was an interesting experience, one that left him impressed with Mayor Pete's commitment to the issue. "For two months we went back and forth with various alternatives and they took this very seriously. They wanted to make sure that whatever they came up with was defensible in terms of cost and the ability to pay for it."

Ultimately, Howard and Pete Buttigieg's team narrowed the focus to three primary options. "One is a catastrophic long-term care program, one of them is enhancing savings, another one is raising wages for home care workers. Of course, the problem with that is it makes the program more expensive!"

Unfortunately, that's where all roads lead—higher taxes and dramatic implications for the national budget. We are at a crossroads as a country. We see the impending crisis, we know what can make a difference, but are unable to choose a path forward.

Learning from Other Countries

Eldercare causes financial and emotional strain for Tightropers and is a source of major economic concern for the US economy. However, the situation is far more acute in other countries—in particular, Japan. Whereas just over 15% of the US is sixty-five or above, Japan's aged are closing in on 30% of the population.

How are countries like Japan dealing with this situation?

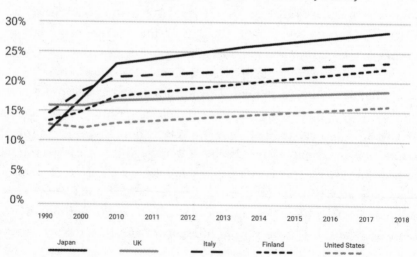

CHART 14.1. Percentage of the Population over 65 by Country[11]

In 2000, Japan introduced Long Term Care Insurance (LTCI) to deal with the growing burdens of eldercare in the country. The premiums are mandatory for everyone over the age of forty and based on income. Users are required to make 10% copayments as a way to minimize overuse of the program.

The program offers a range of institutional-, home-, and community-based services and is accessed through a "care manager" that uses a standardized questionnaire about activities and daily living as well as a report from the enrollee's physician. All of this is reviewed by a local committee that determines the beneficiary's level of need and the corresponding quantity of services. Need levels are reassessed every two years or upon request following a change in health.

Because of the scope of the program, service providers are both for-profit and nonprofit entities. However, the federal government sets the fees for services and reviews them periodically.

It's hard to imagine implementing a program of this cost and breadth in our current political environment, but as the population continues to age, we may not have a choice.

Additionally, Japan leads the rest of the world in the use of technology to support eldercare. The goal of this innovation is to lower the cost to the government by keeping the elderly in their homes longer.

Given sufficient investment and innovation in this area, new monitoring and even robotics innovations could help caregivers stay on top of their duties more cost-effectively. This would also likely improve the quality of care provided. Despite the best intentions of family caregivers, most of them are untrained, which can lead to poor outcomes and even unintentional abuse. Things like incontinence can be a tipping point for caregivers, and tools like ultrasonic bladder sensors can be a boon for avoiding embarrassing accidents.

This is not just a growing national need but a global one. Technology innovation and investment in this area will yield tremendous business opportunities to improve the lives of Tightropers and their aging parents.

15

DEBT THAT STRIPS WEALTH

The dangers of home equity and 401(k) loans for aging Tightropers

- Low-cost credit products such as home equity loans, home equity lines of credit (HELOC), and 401(k) loans are particularly dangerous for aging Tightropers because they often lead to the loss of wealth needed to afford retirement.
- Existing federal rules actually block needed protections for aging Americans.
- Innovative new financial products can provide better solutions.

Boomer Tightropers were lucky in many ways. They didn't face the enormous early-adult costs that Millennials did (especially related to student debt) and had a housing market that provided remarkable appreciation in value—almost anywhere in the country. Also, they experienced more career stability in the past and were usually able to build up their 401(k) savings. That's why Boomers have relatively high "paper" wealth—even Boomer Tightropers. Housing was pretty much a no-brainer for them, and they likely have some retirement savings.

Tapping into the value of their homes or borrowing against their 401(k) savings is incredibly tempting for aging Tightropers facing caregiving responsibilities and expenses. When you have to find a way to pay for your child's tuition or get ramps installed in your house for a loved one with mobility issues, these seem like easy places to turn.

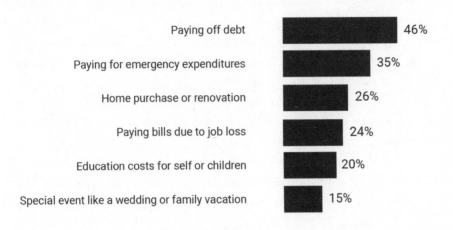

CHART 15.1. Top Reasons for Borrowing from Retirement Savings[1]

Paying off debt — 46%
Paying for emergency expenditures — 35%
Home purchase or renovation — 26%
Paying bills due to job loss — 24%
Education costs for self or children — 20%
Special event like a wedding or family vacation — 15%

Both forms of credit are appealing because they are readily available and carry low or no interest. Isn't this better than running up credit card debt or expensive online loans?

Many traditional credit products can be very effective for young and midlife Americans but aren't appropriate for aging Tightropers. Home equity loans, for instance, can be tremendously helpful for home improvements, debt consolidation, and unexpected expenses. However, they become increasingly dangerous as people age—in particular for Tightropers with limited savings and income volatility. Losing your house because you can't make your debt payments is horrific for anyone, but for aging Tightropers, it is akin to a life sentence.

Any form of credit for Tightropers carries a significantly higher likelihood of loss than for the Safely Stable. Tightropers are normally prone to income volatility, but this is exacerbated in the case of those who may have to reduce work hours due to caregiving responsibilities or health issues.

Whereas someone who is Safely Stable can expect to pay off their loan without missed payments, a Tightroper may face foreclosure if they fall behind on a home equity loan. This is particularly true of home equity lines of credit (HELOC) that can be interest-only for up to ten years. A significant increase in your monthly payments after the first ten years can be a terrible wake-up call for Tightropers on a tight budget.

Reverse mortgages have many of the same pitfalls as HELOCs and home equity loans. Unfortunately, it's all too tempting to take a lump-sum payment from a reverse mortgage and spend it unwisely. Furthermore, there are usually conditions in which the house can be foreclosed on, such as a lengthy period where the house is left empty—potentially due to an illness or disability. Even worse, reverse mortgage contracts typically require immediate repayment on the death of the borrower. If only one spouse's name is on the reverse mortgage contract, when that person dies, their spouse could be left homeless.

Similarly, despite their best intentions to repay a loan against their 401(k), Tightropers have unique challenges. Unexpected expenses start to pile up at the same time income streams start to dry up. Before long, they "default" against themselves and give up on repaying the loan.

At an aggregate level, the problem doesn't seem that bad—defaults for all 401(k) loans are only 10%. However, that number skyrockets to over 85% if the employee leaves their employer before they pay off the loan. For Tightropers, this is just too much of a risk to take with their financial futures.

CHART 15.2. 401(k) Loans and Loan Defaults[2]

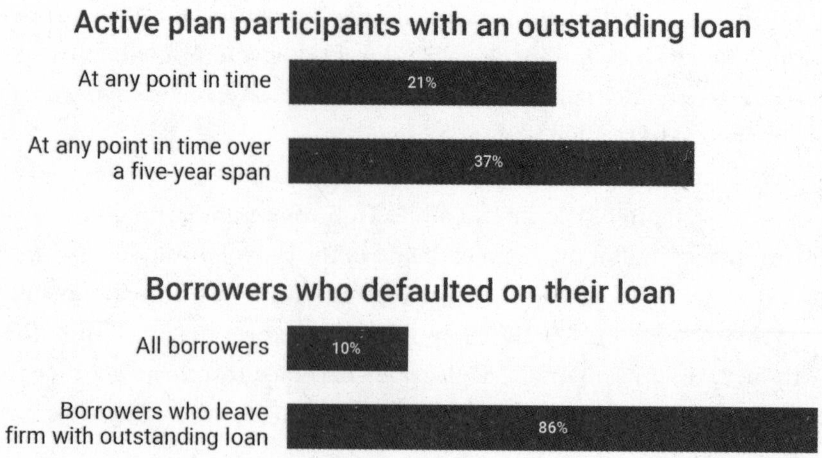

Active plan participants with an outstanding loan

At any point in time	21%
At any point in time over a five-year span	37%

Borrowers who defaulted on their loan

All borrowers	10%
Borrowers who leave firm with outstanding loan	86%

As a society, we can't let at-risk Americans gamble with their houses and retirement savings. The effect of home foreclosures on aging Tightroper families is particularly crushing, and we saw those tragedies play out across the country during the Great Recession.

We have all been told about the problems with payday loans, but they are arguably a better source of credit for many older Tightropers. They may cost a lot, but at least no one loses their house or their retirement savings due to them!

Protecting against Dangerous Credit

Ironically, current federal regulations prevent lenders from discriminating against older people, even if the product is not well-suited to their needs. As a lender, I can refuse a loan to a young applicant because I can prove that they have a greater chance of default, but if a sixty-five-year-old Tightroper wants to get a reverse mortgage or a home equity loan, I can't deny it to her simply because it is not a responsible loan product for her financial situation.

Regulators need to rethink federal regulations to provide additional protections for aging Tightropers. In particular, I believe that all debt products that take a security interest in personal property or retirement savings should have significantly more limitations for people in their sixties and beyond. It should be much harder for them to get these kinds of loans, and it should be much harder for lenders to foreclose on them. We already have special protections for members of the military and their families—why not for older Americans as well?

How Financial Innovation Can Help

So what's the answer for aging Tightropers who want to monetize the value of what is the only real source of wealth for the majority of Americans— their homes?

When I spoke with Ron Suber, called "the Godfather of Fintech," he told me that financial technology innovators were beginning to address this opportunity.

"This is a problem that's facing millions of Americans. They bought their house ten or twenty years ago, have made payments, and now it's their biggest asset," said Ron. "Unfortunately, it's also a mostly illiquid asset. Refinancing will generate fees and additional interest payments but selling the house and moving isn't an option either."

The interesting idea that some Fintech innovators are trying, says Ron, is "a shift from debt to equity" to unlock the value of the house.

Here's an example. Let's say you purchased your home for $200,000 fifteen years ago and still owe $100,000, but the home is now worth $400,000. Instead of giving you risky debt, these innovators are offering cash for an equity position in your house. "They will pay you $40,000 for 10% of the house," explains Ron. "The bank is still there—it has first position—but when you or your offspring ultimately sell the property, the investor will receive 10% of the proceeds."

Companies like **Haus** are pioneering this type of offering. This is the type of financial innovation that can make a difference for older Tightropers and can create economic value for investors. Homeowners don't take on additional debt and they don't pay exorbitant fees, but investors get to share in the appreciation of the property while benefiting from the homeowner's upkeep of the property.

Granted, this isn't a solution for everyone—what is?—but regulators need to be open to and encourage a broad set of new innovative approaches that are better suited for aging Tightropers.

16

WAYS TO REINFORCE AND REIMBURSE BEFORE RETIREMENT

Tightropers can't afford to wait

- Tightropers don't mind working longer—but employers need to change.
- Expanding the earned-income tax credit to provide benefits and contribute to retirement savings for unpaid caregivers can reward the sacrifices Tightropers made for their families and loved ones.
- New automated financial tools and robo-advisors developed for Tightropers can help future generations achieve a more secure retirement.

L istening to the stories of aging Tightropers invariably brings a sense of humility, admiration, and deep concern. After full lives, they find themselves struggling rather than easing into a comfortable retirement. Yet they never stop worrying about and sacrificing for their families, even as they see their own nest eggs evaporate.

Furthermore, aging Tightropers are unceasingly pragmatic. They rarely expect a financial *deus ex machina* from the government. They tend to take responsibility for their lives and the decisions they have made.

That doesn't mean they aren't frustrated and afraid. They see the coming financial challenges and don't know exactly how they'll get by. They'll take any help they can get.

Flexible Work for Lifelong Employment

We often think that "you can't teach an old dog new tricks." That type of stereotyping leads us to discount the ongoing contributions of Tightropers in their sixties and beyond. Americans are living longer and are healthier than ever before. The answer for many isn't governmental programs and spending, but continued involvement in the workforce.

Employers can lead the charge by redefining final career stages and inventing new ways to hire and employ those past the traditional retirement age. While flexible work schedules are no panacea for caregiving and health issues, they make a huge difference in supporting an aging workforce. In many ways, older workers and Millennials want the same latitude to work when they want and where they want, with one big difference: Baby Boomers have proven their ability to deliver results, while young workers are still establishing their track records.

Forced retirement ages have historically been something that unions and others fought for. This no longer makes sense. Instead of limiting themselves to the parameters implied by outdated workplace regulations, employers need to figure out fresh ways to continue employing older workers. Regulators also have a role in supporting these changes. They will need to update Social Security, Medicare, pension, and tax-advantaged savings systems, for Tightropers especially, to continue working as long as they want.

Rewarding the Sacrifices of Aging Caregivers

The typical caregiver is a woman in her fifties. According to Howard Gleckman at the Urban-Brookings Tax Policy Center, if she leaves her job to care for a parent or disabled adult child, "studies suggest she will forego somewhere between $200,000 and $300,000 in lifetime income." Given that caregiving is a documented neutron bomb to lifelong earnings, especially for women, why not find ways to compensate them for their sacrifices and enable them to catch up financially?

Adjusting the earned-income tax credit to correct for unpaid eldercare is one possible answer. There have been numerous proposals to enhance and expand the EITC, usually with bold acronyms like LIFT ("Livable Income for Families Today"), introduced by then-Senator Kamala Harris, and GAIN ("Grow American Income Now"), introduced by Senator Sherrod Brown and Representative Ro Khanna. However, the one that provides for the needs of unpaid caregivers is called the EITC Modernization Act, sponsored by Representative Bonnie Watson Coleman.

Expanding the EITC makes a lot of sense. According to a study by the AARP Public Policy Institute, the value of unpaid care work in the US is nearly $500 billion a year.[1] This is more than the cost of all paid home care and Medicaid spending combined.

However, merely providing a cash EITC payout annually doesn't address the fundamental problem. Tightropers are incredibly savvy at finding ways to get by with limited income, but they struggle to put money away for retirement or in case of a financial emergency. If this expanded EITC program simply pays caregivers for their labor, the money would likely be spent, rather than saved for retirement.

Rather than give caregivers an annual lump sum payment, the way traditional EITC benefits are provided, a more beneficial modification of the EITC would be to treat any benefits for unpaid caregivers like contributions to Social Security. The central issue for aging Tightropers is what will happen to them when they are no longer able to work. We need to address this by helping them build up protected savings while they still can.

Such a policy adjustment would disproportionately benefit women, as it should. Women live longer than men and must plan differently for their careers, health care, caregiving, investments, and withdrawals. Crafting gender-specific policies corrects the gender-blind approach that currently punishes women who take on family caregiving obligations.

This isn't to say it would be easy. "You would get a lot of abuse," says Howard. "We already struggle with Medicare fraud and this would have the same problems."

Furthermore, the political obstacles would be immense. Howard is rightly skeptical from his experience in Washington, DC. "I've heard politicians say to me that I'm nuts if I think I can get a tax implemented today for a benefit that people won't get for thirty to forty years."

However, this issue won't fix itself. Caregivers are sacrificing earnings and decimating savings, which will lead to a predictable result. In fact, many sources are already predicting that we will face a retirement "crisis" in the next few years. With median savings in 401(k) accounts for people sixty-five and older dropping to a measly $58,035,[2] how will aging Tightropers survive without massive new benefits programs? As a nation, we can't afford to kick the can on this issue any longer.

Make Financial Planning Real— and Yield Better Results

Aging Tightropers on the verge of retirement need help now. Realistically, they can only earn so much more in their lifetimes and their savings can only be enhanced so much. But we also need to think about the needs of future generations as they retire.

Everybody knows they should save. Everybody knows that what they don't save today won't be available tomorrow.

But theoretical statements and generic platitudes don't motivate, much less inspire, people to save, invest, and put tomorrow ahead of today.

What does work? Envisioning your "future self" living very specific consequences of today's decisions. Let's say your idea of an ideal retirement is a blend of travel, volunteering, and birdwatching. You'll be much more motivated to control household living expenses and save more if you can connect the dots between today's decisions and the benefits for your "future self."

Tightropers know about budgeting, credit rules, and cash flow—often more than the Safely Stable. But when you're on the Tightrope, you focus on one step at a time. You balance, plot, and plan that next step. Getting to the end of the Tightrope is outside your field of vision. You're just trying not to fall.

The American financial planning machine is oriented toward the far future, as anticipated by the Safely Stable. The Safely Stable already are rewarding themselves for their hard work. They do not have to play mind games to motivate themselves to save—they are already taking vacations, volunteering, and birdwatching. For the Safely Stable, retirement is a continuation of the good life, not its start.

For Tightropers, though, cold numbers don't motivate. Rich hopes do. The more immediate, detailed, and personal the potential payoff, the easier it is to resist borrowing from your 401(k) account to pay for your child's college semester abroad.

As an example, weddings have become an incredible drain on families wanting to provide the best for their children. Negotiating a more modest wedding for your daughter might be a challenge in the near-term, but can lead to more time with that daughter's children in the future if you don't have to work longer to pay yourself back.

This sort of context and communication can make a world of difference. Translating tedious, data-choked communications into engaging coaching and financial forecasting sessions could make a tremendous difference in outcomes for Tightropers but is extremely challenging. Most financial planners and academics tend to favor dry, unexciting approaches based on simplistic assumptions about how our lives will proceed.

It's easy to see why Tightropers don't connect with these approaches. Even the academic exercise of the "miracle of compound interest" delivers unimpressive results for the first two decades. And in the real world, taxes, inflation, and investment fees all erode the actual results of the supposed financial miracle.

On the other hand, there is the temptation for Fintech app designers to use gimmicks and "gamification" to attempt to trick customers into doing the "right" thing. These often condescending approaches are off-putting to the people they are intended for. Tightropers expect to be treated like adults. Silicon Valley innovators have not completely cracked the code for delivering engaging content and tools that don't infantilize people yet.

I remain optimistic, however. Fintech innovation has the potential to be far more effective than traditional approaches for coaching a new generation of Tightropers toward a safe and secure retirement. Products like **Robin Hood**, **Acorns**, and others have demystified investing for millions of consumers, and they are just the start.

By listening to Tightropers—and avoiding condescending approaches—innovators can develop products that will support a lifetime of wealth accumulation and help future generations of Americans afford a secure retirement.

SECTION 5

Building a Sustainable Safety Net

17

HOW GOVERNMENT CAN HELP

The nine most terrifying words

- Retiring Tightropers will bankrupt the economy unless something is done.
- There are ways the government can help without creating unintended consequences.
- Tightropers need programs that support savings and provide a safety net in between jobs.
- Financial services providers need regulatory support to responsibly serve Tightropers.

America can't afford Tightropers.

Escalating income instability and eroding personal savings have triggered a slowly accelerating financial landslide. People don't save for today, never mind for retirement. This landslide is picking up speed as Baby Boomers retire, and threatens to overwhelm the financial stability of a whole generation as Social Security and Medicare are stretched to the breaking point. The damage will cascade to the next generations, too, which are even less prepared than Baby Boomers to fund their retirements. The fact that two-thirds of all adults under the age of thirty-eight (i.e., Millennials) have no retirement savings is a harbinger of the coming crisis.

Politicians from both parties are beginning to speak more about the needs and financial stresses facing American Tightropers who are concerned about an impending recession or even depression. But talking isn't doing. Saying "I have a plan for it" isn't enough. Tightropers need real change that will improve their lives, not unrealistic or unworkable policy proposals.

No Going Back

President Trump's famous campaign promise to "Make America Great Again" is in many ways a wish to take the country back to a time before the economic transformations that created so many Tightropers. And from the political left, we are told that we need to renew "the social contracts that once bound employers, families, and government"[1] to reduce economic fragility.

Unfortunately, the rising instability that fueled the growth of Tightropers in this country is not going away any time soon. It's going to get worse.

The COVID-19 pandemic made it painfully clear to people at every income level how quickly things can change and how little control we really have over our financial lives. Whether we like it or not, the genie of economic disruption is out of the bottle and is here to stay.

Tightropers need better support to manage the rapid changes and dislocations of modern life. Unfortunately, political gridlock has made policy legislation harder than ever to pass. Rising partisanship threatens even the most obvious and uncontroversial improvements to the lives of Tightropers.

The time for change is now. We need policy recommendations that recognize the new economic realities and that can win bipartisan support. The following recommendations will help Tightropers improve their personal safety nets, reduce the risks of using credit, and help jumpstart the private sector to provide better tools and services.

Recommendations That Can Move Tightropers to Solid Ground

Ronald Reagan famously said, "the most terrifying nine words in the English language are: 'I'm from the government and I'm here to help.'"

Coming up with recommendations for public policy, regulatory, and legislative change is fraught with difficulty. There is always a temptation to wave the magic wand of massive spending programs to solve issues. Simplistic proposals of this sort always seem very bold, despite the fact that they have no chance of actually being implemented, or if implemented, bring the risk of significant unintended consequences. On the other hand, overly incremental measures won't actually make a difference.

Fortunately, I know Aaron Klein in Washington, DC, through a working group that the CFPB established to develop recommendations for rules related to high-cost lending. The CFPB bravely sought advice from a wide group of stakeholders including both lenders and consumer advocates and they asked Aaron to help the group find common ground. Despite the challenging nature of the assignment (much like "herding cats," according to Aaron), he was successful in getting us to agree on a series of ambitious recommendations for improving consumer protections while preserving access to needed credit.

Aaron has incredible credentials as a nonpartisan thinker on financial services issues. He is a fellow at the Brookings Institute in Economic Studies and is the policy director of the Center on Regulation and Markets. Previously, he served at the Treasury Department as Deputy Assistant Secretary for Economic Policy and as the Chief Economist of the Senate Banking, Housing and Urban Affairs Committee. He worked on financial regulatory reform issues including drafting and helping secure passage of the Dodd-Frank Wall Street Reform and Consumer Protection Act of 2010.

I was fortunate to get some of his time to talk through a wide range of ideas about what the government could do to help Tightropers in these polarized times.

The following are some straightforward, common-sense recommendations that I believe will make a difference in the lives of Tightropers and should not be subject to the fierce partisanship that has made legislative efforts so difficult. Aaron certainly doesn't agree with all of them (and should not be blamed for any of my ideas), but he was instrumental in helping me consider the pros and cons of each.

Help Tightropers Build Emergency Savings

The first priority is to help Tightropers build emergency savings. Why? Because most financial setbacks Tightropers face can be solved with less than a few thousand dollars. Whether the problem is a temporary reduction in wages, a broken washer or dryer, new tires, or a trip to the veterinarian, access to emergency savings helps Tightropers avoid taking out debt or dipping into retirement savings.

Unfortunately, most governmental and employer savings programs like IRAs and 401(k)s are terrible for small-dollar financial emergencies. In fact, due to their high penalties for early withdrawal, they can be more expensive than payday loans if used for short-term needs.

Furthermore, getting access to 401(k) or IRA savings requires significant paperwork and it can take weeks to receive the needed funds from the plan administrator. Tightropers need hassle-free access to savings in minutes, not weeks.

401(k) and IRA programs need to be modified to support the real-world financial needs of Tightropers. Instead of a one-size-fits-all retirement plan, government-sponsored savings programs should have two components. The primary component should be (as today) focused on long-term retirement savings. However, a new component of these programs should be accessible as an alternative to short-term borrowing—an Emergency Savings Account.

Funds allocated to long-term retirement savings can work as they do today. They are administered and invested by plan administrators and have penalties for early withdrawal. However, Tightropers should be able to allocate up to $5,000 of their 401(k) and/or IRA into an Emergency Savings Account that can be accessed at any time and with minimal paperwork.

If the Tightroper has a short-term financial need, instead of getting credit or asking friends or family, they can make a draw on their Emergency Savings Account. This would be processed online instantly, and the requested funds electronically pushed into the bank account linked to the 401(k) or IRA. Later, the Emergency Savings Account would be replenished by either higher payroll withholdings for a period of time or a reduction in their annual tax refund.

Aaron agrees that Tightropers need emergency savings to avoid high-interest credit products, but is worried about linking it to retirement savings. "What if they don't repay it? They would get less retirement benefits, so all we are going to do is increase poverty among the elderly," he stated. "That's a horrible idea—why not just offer people a separate product for that specific purpose?"

Whether the Emergency Savings Account is directly linked to a retirement account or a separate fund, the creation of a Federal Emergency Savings Account isn't a panacea. People who experience long-term loss of income or continuing high expenses will need another solution. However, Emergency Savings Accounts will reduce barriers for Tightropers to contribute to 401(k)s and IRAs and will significantly limit their need for short-term credit products, potentially saving them billions in interest charges.

Ensure a Clear Roadmap to Retirement

The US government actually does a lot to encourage retirement savings. There are a variety of 401(k) and IRA plans that provide strong tax benefits for consumers who save for retirement. They all basically work the same way—you can put pretax income into them and avoid or delay paying taxes until retirement while they appreciate in value.

For consumers who work at companies that match 401(k) contributions, the deal is pretty unbeatable. It's essentially free money.

Unfortunately, employee contribution rates remain low even with matching plans. Only 55% of the workforce has access to a 401(k) plan and of those, nearly one-third of employees don't participate.[2] What's going on—who wouldn't take "free money?"

Part of the problem with governmental retirement savings programs is that they disproportionately benefit high earners. "What's the incentive for contributing to your IRA?" Aaron asked. "The incentive is what you save on your marginal tax rate—well we have a progressive marginal tax system so it's less valuable to the people who most need to save."

When Tightropers elect not to contribute to 401(k)s and IRAs, they aren't necessarily doing the wrong thing. Tightropers are continually aware of their financial vulnerability. With limited cash savings and damaged credit scores, which can preclude access to reasonably priced credit in times of need, they are understandably reluctant to lock up income in a 401(k) or IRA that can't be used in an emergency.

Aaron believes we need a stronger incentive for lower-income Tightropers than merely a reduction in taxes. He suggests "maybe we need a matched savings component or even start it out with $100 at birth—but it's going to take more than a tax break to get the behavior change that's needed."

I think Aaron is right. We all win when aging Tightropers have saved for retirement. But their needs are not the same as the Safely Stable and we should create new incentives for Tightropers to save and protect those savings from being eroded.

It's great that many employers have 401(k) matching programs, but let's face it, they are declining in relevance as we shift toward a gig economy and as employers increase the level of automation and the use of offshore labor. It's time for the government to step in.

All earnings—from both steady jobs and gig work—should come with a forced savings component and we should help Tightropers get the most from that savings by providing some level of matching based on income level. Unlike our current programs that provide the most benefit to the wealthy, we need new programs that specifically focus on Tightropers and provide special incentives for their unique needs.

Additionally, as we discussed, aging Tightropers are often caregivers and lose potential earnings providing for their families and loved ones. Because of the high societal benefit of these sacrifices, we should compensate caregivers by continuing to contribute to retirement savings. This compensation will be less than they could have made if they had stayed in the workforce, but any ongoing retirement contributions will make a huge impact on the ability of aging Tightropers to comfortably retire without requiring ongoing public assistance.

And of course, one of the best ways to ensure that Tightropers retain their retirement savings is by supporting them when they face job loss—especially due to factors outside their control such as COVID-19. We need to improve the essential safety nets for Tightropers as they retool and transition from one job or career to the next. This will require improved unemployment benefits, healthcare during unemployment, rent support and credit forbearance. Since these programs are targeted at people facing the greatest hardship, they will give people a sense of stability and support—at acceptable cost—as they prepare for the next stage of their working lives.

Protect Tightropers from Punitive Credit Products

Enhancing savings is important but not the whole answer. Many Tightropers may not build enough savings or face a more significant financial setback that requires them to use credit. As we have emphasized throughout this book, access to credit is an important safety net for those facing problems stemming from income volatility or unexpected expenses, and even high-cost credit products can be a smart alternative for many real-world situations.

Unfortunately, many of the credit products that are widely available to Tightropers pose significant risks to consumers and need to be changed, in particular, those that have punitive fees, require collateral to secure small-dollar credit, or use legal action to aggressively collect on the debt.

Here's why.

Traditional "prime"-oriented credit products assume that most customers will have no problem repaying them and that those who struggle with repayment just need the threat of additional fees to get back on track. Hence, they have very low stated APRs, but lots of fees and even penalty interest if borrowers fall behind on payments. Even worse, many states allow lenders to sue borrowers for nonpayment in court.

This structure has worked adequately for "prime" borrowers for a hundred years or so, but is exactly the wrong approach for Tightropers.

Tightropers are much more likely to struggle to make on-time payments. And once a Tightroper falls behind with their payments, adding on penalty fees and higher interest rates makes it nearly impossible to repay the loan.

Tightropers need credit that comes with a "safety net" in case of repayment difficulty.

Safety Net Credit won't have any punitive fees such as late fees, returned payment fees, or penalty interest. Nor will the customer be required to pledge collateral. The stated APR of credit to Tightropers should reflect the risk of the customer and not require additional fees or the potential loss of belongings to punish those who struggle with debt payments.

And of course, taking a Tightroper to court to collect on nonpayment creates incredible financial and emotional stresses and is tantamount to the cruelties of the debtors prisons of the eighteenth and nineteenth centuries. This practice may be justifiable for larger loans made to customers with significant financial resources or in cases of clear fraud. However, lawsuits are an abusive practice if they are used to collect on small-dollar loans to people with a high likelihood of default.

Aging Tightropers need special protections against products that work well for younger people. Products like home equity lines of credit and 401(k) loans can be useful for those who can expect a long lifetime of earnings, but are reckless for those nearing retirement. The current federal lending laws that are meant to protect older people against discrimination actually leave them vulnerable to products that are most dangerous at this period of life. We need age-based federal regulation that ensures people receive the most appropriate credit products for their individual needs.

Access to credit for nonprime Americans is essential but needs additional safeguards. That way, consumers can receive the benefits of credit while having "training wheels" to avoid it getting out of control.

Encourage Financial Innovation for Tightropers

I've highlighted some of the problems with many credit products offered to Tightropers.

These products have flourished, not because they are universally loved by customers, but because in many cases they are the only options available to Tightropers. Tightropers are often grateful for any form of credit—but don't they deserve better?

The primary obstacles to successful financial innovation are the current lending laws and regulatory environment. They are needlessly complex, outdated, and not conducive to technology-based solutions. Innovators need simpler rules and more regulatory clarity to justify their investment.

A great place to start is by streamlining the byzantine and often bizarre state-by-state regulatory structure that nonbank lenders must navigate.

For instance, several states still require lenders to have branch locations, which prevent lower-cost, online providers from entering the state. Texas has created an odd loophole where lenders can't charge more than 10%, but "Credit Service Organizations" (CSOs) can charge as much as they like for finding a lender for the customer. This has meant that Texas payday lenders simply charge triple-digit rates as CSOs rather than as direct lenders. And one of the oddest of all is Wisconsin's "tattletale" law, which requires lenders to notify the spouse of each borrower about the existence of any new debt—presumably so the spouse can prevent it. These types of state-specific regulatory peculiarities make it expensive and complicated to operate across the United States.

It's hard to imagine another industry that is saddled with as many state-specific restrictions as financial services. Ironically, all of these state rules and regulations have almost no impact on the borrowing behavior and products used by most Americans since the overwhelming majority of credit is provided by national banks who aren't subject to these rules. This situation makes no sense and merely restricts much-needed innovation by nonbank lenders.

The other problem is the antiquated nature of many of the federal lending laws. Most of them were drafted long before the advent of personal computers and cellphones and make it extremely difficult to leverage the power of new data sources and sophisticated analytical techniques for underwriting Tightropers.

"We have a '70s-era list of protected classes that are deeply inconsistent across financial products," Aaron says. "You can use gender and age for pricing car insurance—particularly for teenage males—but if you do the same thing with credit decisions you go directly to jail." As a CEO in this industry, I can confirm this is an issue that lenders take very seriously—no one wants to push the needle on federal lending law.

Aaron highlights TV viewership as an example of regulations not keeping up with the times. "Would you rather lend to someone who watches Shark Tank or someone who watches the Kardashians? I'm pretty sure one would be a better risk than the other, but most regulators would be very uncomfortable with that lending criteria." They would be primarily concerned that using TV preferences would lead to what is called a "disparate impact," where the underlying data inadvertently discriminates against a protected class.

This hypothetical situation becomes increasingly real as new data sources become widely available. Lenders now have access to customers' bank account transactions, favorite TV shows, hobbies, fitness routines, social media usage, eating habits, and dating preferences. And with new machine-learning analytical techniques, they can be rapidly analyzed and easily built into powerful scores that could lower the cost of credit for millions of Tightropers.

Regulators need to provide clarity for innovators and technologists on how to leverage advanced analytical techniques like machine-learning and alternative data sources without inadvertently running afoul of lending laws. The Consumer Financial Protection Bureau has recognized this need but has only offered up "no-action letters" that would theoretically protect innovators against regulatory fines. To date, they have only issued one "no-action" letter. That's not enough.

Federal regulators—whether at the CFPB, FDIC, or OCC—need to commit to the hard work of updating federal lending regulations for a new era. Technology can help Tightropers by providing better options, but without regulatory clarity, innovators can't make the investments necessary to achieve this goal.

Get Banks to Say "Yes" Again to Tightropers

Millions of Americans deposit money with banks that won't return the favor by lending to them.

Over the past decades, banks failed to comprehend the changing economic realities in this country, and consequently failed to innovate. This situation was exacerbated by regulatory actions (many in response to the Great Recession) that caused banks to tighten credit standards and pull back even further from people with less than perfect credit. Now banks are no longer the preferred source of personal credit for nearly half of Americans.

Ironically, the regulatory pressure that drove this situation was based on an inaccurate assessment of the riskiness of subprime lending. It turns out

that Tightropers are actually LESS impacted by recessions and other periods of economic stress than the Safely Stable.

Data provided by the credit bureau TransUnion shows that for unsecured personal credit, although credit scores are highly correlated with
overall loss rates, they are negatively correlated with the volatility in loss
rates due to macroeconomic conditions. This means that while Tightropers are more likely to default on their loans than the Safely Stable, their
default rates will remain more consistent in both good times and bad. As
long as banks correctly price their credit based on customer riskiness, they
are actually better off in a recession if they lend to Tightropers who "always live in a recession."[3]

Having spoken with dozens of bank executives about the plight of
Tightropers, I can attest that they want to start lending to their customers
again. They see that their customers are going to payday lenders and other
nonbank providers and want to offer a better alternative. They also want
to grow profits and recognize that Tightropers represent a vast, underserved demographic. They just don't know how to serve them without
taking on risk and massive technology investment.

One way to jump-start this process is for banks to partner with financial
technology companies. Banks have deep customer relationships, deposi-
tory relationships, regulatory advantages, and essentially free cost of capital. Fintech innovators are nimble, understand technology, and can
rapidly prototype and test new financial products.

So far, banks have been tentative about these partnerships and regulators and consumer groups have occasionally criticized them. But it
shouldn't be that way. As Bill Isaac, former Chairman of the FDIC, pro-
claimed in a *Wall Street Journal* article he coauthored with me in 2017,
"Fintech innovators are not the enemy."[4] He continued that "most banks
outsource the technology used in branch systems and for support of their
core products. Fintech innovators should be encouraged to work with
banks, not compete against them." If properly encouraged and managed,
bank-Fintech partnerships have the potential to go together like "choco-
late and peanut butter" and could help banks return to their original
mission as the primary financial institution of mainstream Americans.

Banks need to get back in the game, but it's unrealistic to think they
will do so without a hard push. I believe we need a new and improved

Community Reinvestment Act (CRA) that will encourage and provide safeguards for banks who serve Tightropers.

The current CRA is woefully outdated. It was created to make sure that banks had physical branches in low-income neighborhoods. However, in a world with ATMs in every convenience store and a banking app on every phone, who needs branches? Even worse, CRA merely encourages banks to provide the traditional banking services that fit "prime" Americans rather than Tightropers. We need to fundamentally rethink the objectives of CRA to recognize that Tightropers need services, not branches, and to delineate a new generation of bank products for Americans living paycheck to paycheck.

Federal protections for banks, along with FDIC insurance, represent a major subsidy by taxpayers for the thousands of US banks. As a result, they should not be standing on the sidelines while Tightropers struggle with financial setbacks and inferior credit options.

An example of a bank credit product that fits the demands of Tightropers is US Bank's Simple Loan product. This product provides up to $1,000 in credit to account holders. It is approved and funded quickly with minimal paperwork and repaid rapidly over three months. It has a high APR of 70% to 88% to cover costs and defaults, but no punitive fees. Also, successful payments are reported to credit bureaus to help borrowers rebuild their credit. While many consumer advocates find the costs high, it is well-suited to the needs of Tightropers and yields sufficient returns to the bank to justify offering it broadly.

Aaron Klein is more pessimistic about changes to the CRA. "CRA is not as powerful a tool as many people on both sides of the issue make it out to be. A bigger obstacle to community banks lending to Tightropers is that they have no way to sell that loan off of their balance sheet so the regulators penalize them with higher capital requirements."

As usual, Aaron makes an important point. We can't ignore the additional risks that are inherent in lending to Tightropers. It will also be essential to help smaller banks diversify their credit risk with a thriving ecosystem of loan originators and "syndicators" who can buy and sell these loans to ensure individual banks are safe and sound.

THERE HAS NEVER been a more critical time to make meaningful policy change that will benefit Tightropers. COVID-19 demonstrated the urgency of the need, but also the potential wastefulness of federal programs that aren't well-designed and implemented. Will policy makers and legislators have the courage to put aside political rhetoric to help Tightropers build safety nets and have a fighting chance at comfortable retirements?

Time will tell.

18

HOW GOVERNMENT
CAN MAKE THINGS WORSE

Distracting, dangerous, and dumb policy ideas

- Most proposed policy solutions won't help.
- Some may even make matters worse.
- Be careful of unintended consequences.

Policymakers and politicians want to make a positive difference for Americans. Despite the cynicism many feel, those inside the Beltway and in state capitals are there largely because they care deeply about this country and are committed to making it better.

However, most of the widely discussed policy initiatives are a distraction to the important changes that could improve the financial well-being of millions of Tightropers. Or they could make things worse. Regulators and legislators need to sidestep the following dubious approaches.

Grandiose Social Programs and Giveaways

This book has attempted to make the case that the rise in financial instability that has turned half of this country into Tightropers is one of the top policy (and moral) imperatives of our time. It should be clear that we need to make this issue a priority and mobilize government and private sector forces to improve the situation.

So why am I not proposing massive spending programs and wealth re-distribution programs to bring about radical change?

Unfortunately, these big programs rarely get implemented and when they do, they often have significant unanticipated consequences. As a re-sult, I believe they should be a last resort to this crisis, not the first one, and are an unnecessary distraction to more realistic proposals.

Politicians love big, ambitious policy initiatives. Sweeping change sounds great on the campaign trail, generates interesting talking points, spurs the faithful, and attracts media coverage. Inevitably, these big ideas struggle to gain meaningful legislative traction and are doused by post-election realities. Unfortunately, the "visionary" campaign promises dis-tract the conversation from pragmatic alternatives that could achieve bipartisan support and near-term implementation.

While it is undoubtedly true that eliminating Tightropers' expenses related to healthcare, education, and childcare or the creation of a "uni-versal basic income" would have a positive impact on financial stability, the details of implementing these changes are unavoidably challenging. Issues like how to maintain incentives for cost control and quality are nontrivial and typically cause real-world legislation to bog down. Also, many of the ideas (e.g., free tuition) end up benefiting wealthier Americans more than Tightropers.

As an example, one of the most important pieces of legislation in the twentieth century was the Higher Education Act of 1972. It created Sallie Mae to provide broad access to student loans and encourage more Amer-icans to go to college. Although brilliant in principle, according to its primary architect, Alice Rivlin, it created "perverse incentives" for col-leges, which resulted in a nearly 1500% increase in tuition costs (adjusted for inflation) since 1978—twice the price increase of healthcare over the same period and nearly five times the increase in the overall price index. It's no wonder that Ms. Rivlin looks back and now believes that "we un-leashed a monster."[1]

This isn't to say that ambitious and expensive legislation isn't occasion-ally required and wouldn't have value. It's just that we should be realistic about the likelihood of enactment and be skeptical about the benefits. Tightropers can't afford to wait for the "perfect" solution (even if there was one)—they need "good" solutions that will make a difference in their lives right away.

Furthermore, the top "1%" isn't realistically capable of paying for all of these new entitlement programs. Instead, these would likely require significant tax increases on the middle class, which create additional financial stress on those Americans—potentially creating even more Tightropers than today. And with tax revenues rapidly drying up due to the economic impacts of COVID-19, this simply isn't sustainable.

One Exception—Healthcare Reform

I am skeptical of ambitious legislative proposals because they rarely deliver the anticipated benefits and they often create long-term problems. However, even with those caveats, something needs to be done about healthcare.

Medical problems and the expenses and income disruptions they bring are devastating to Tightropers. Whether a major illness or a minor procedure, and whether it happens to the Tightroper or a loved one, healthcare bills can quickly spiral out of control and mire Tightropers in a never-ending web of debt and mounting expenses.

As highlighted earlier in this book, three-quarters of Tightropers who have significant medical bills also experience an income drop, severely complicating their ability to manage and cover medical expenses. And the negative impacts of health problems don't stop with the sick or injured person. Caregiving by loved ones can take a significant financial toll on families, potentially undermining their own well-being and touching off another round of medical care.

This issue is not going away. The COVID-19 pandemic proved that our healthcare system is even more flawed than we realized. Fixing it will result in financial reform as well as healthcare reform and is the most important policy mandate for this country.

History tells us progress won't be easy. In the 1990s, Bill Clinton was unable to pass any meaningful healthcare reform despite making it a key policy imperative. Not until 2012, with control of the presidency and both the House and Senate, were the Democrats able to pass the deeply flawed

Affordable Care Act that became known as Obamacare. And despite that sweeping and hotly contested legislation, the financial impact of medical costs and disruption on the lives of Tightropers hasn't improved measurably. In fact, out of pocket medical expenses for Americans have actually gone up significantly since the enactment of the Affordable Care Act.[2]

It is not in the scope of this book to examine the failures of Obamacare or propose alternative approaches. However, it is important to highlight how much more we need to do about healthcare in this country if we want to make a real difference in the lives of average Americans, Tightropers in particular.

Interest-Rate Caps

Rate caps are popular with many consumer advocates.

It's easy to see why. The triple-digit annual percentage rates of payday and title lenders are eye-popping and evoke an almost primal response that "something must be done." Such rates appear inherently predatory. The case for usury limits seems self-evident.

That is, unless you rely on credit as a safety net.

As you have already heard from Tightropers, they have limited resources to weather financial setbacks. Without significant savings, job loss, reduction in income, or an unexpected expense can cause tremendous stress, and credit can be an important tool to manage through cash shortfalls. Lacking access to credit can lead to even worse situations—like being unable to repair your car and get to work.

Savings is certainly the best solution for Tightropers, but when that runs out, credit is the only realistic alternative. Few can turn to friends and family, whose resources are often equally thin. Asking for charity is either not an option or is viewed as demeaning. Nor do Tightropers have the option of going to a bank or credit union for a loan. They know that those financial institutions stopped serving people like them long ago.

So why are rates high? Why hasn't competition driven down the rates to this growing segment of consumers?

It's no surprise—their financial instability makes them a bad credit risk. Hence, rate caps only serve to reduce access to credit and eliminate one of the most important ways that millions of Tightropers manage through temporary financial setbacks.

Tightropers need and deserve protection against financial products that can create a cycle of debt or have outsized risks to borrowers. As stated throughout this book, I strongly believe that increased protections and what I call "Safety Net" credit products are essential. However, arbitrary rate caps are counterproductive.

Tightropers themselves are best suited to determining whether the cost of credit can be justified given their other concerns and financial needs. Who would second-guess a parent who took out a payday loan if it was the only way to pay for their child's visit to the doctor?

Not all consumer advocates believe in ultralow rate caps on credit. Nick Bourke, director of consumer finance at the Pew Charitable Trusts, has thought deeply about this subject. We've been on several panels together on topics in consumer lending and he is someone I have a lot of respect for (although we don't see eye to eye on everything). While he strongly believes in expanded consumer protections and a greater focus on loan affordability, he recognizes the need for credit and has publicly applauded the emergence of products like US Bank's 80% Simple Loan product. "It's a great first step" and a "game-changer," Mr. Bourke said.[3]

I recognize that, unfortunately, rate caps continue to gain momentum among well-meaning legislators and consumer groups. For those who still believe in rate caps despite the data and Tightroper stories in this book, I would encourage them to tier the rate caps by loan amount. It is far more expensive (per dollar lent) to offer a small-dollar, short-term loan than a mortgage, and the rates need to reflect this. In order to preserve access to credit for Tightropers, a small-dollar loan should have a much higher acceptable interest rate than a higher dollar one.

The Economics of Lending to Tightropers

The challenge of providing credit to Tightropers extends beyond just the risk of loss. The typical financial shortfalls that impact Tightropers are best served by short-term, small-dollar credit that can be funded quickly and without a great deal of paperwork and hassle. These are difficult to provide profitably at a low cost.

This is my business, so let me unpack the cost of a $1,000 loan that will be repaid over six months or less.

Marketing isn't free. Whether you are a nonprofit, a bank, or an online lender, it costs money to make consumers aware of your products and services and be willing to try them out. There is significant cost involved whether the lender has brick and mortar stores to attract drive-by traffic or uses the internet or direct mail campaigns to reach consumers. On average, Google charges about $18 every time someone clicks on your listing if you bid on premium keywords like "loan" (although my marketing team has seen prices spike over $70 per click!). And large customer aggregators in the credit space such as Credit Karma can charge more than $200 for every customer they send to prospective lenders. It takes a lot of skill and experience to keep marketing costs under $200 per new customer at scale.

Underwriting Tightropers is complicated and high stakes. It can also be expensive. Getting data from the various "Big Three" credit bureaus (TransUnion, Experian, and Equifax) and "alternative" credit bureaus (such as Clarity, Factor Trust, or Teletrack), not to mention fraud data vendors (e.g., Iovation, IDology) and internal underwriting and fraud staff, can cost upwards of $20 per customer (assuming the lender funds about one in five applicants).

Customer service and loan servicing tend to add up—especially for nonprime credit. Customers typically need more assistance with applying and making payments. Let's assume servicing costs of $5 per month for each customer.

Between marketing, underwriting costs, and servicing costs, the average lender will spend over $250 to provide credit to a Tightroper (whether or not they ever repay the loan). If you factor in losses from defaulted loans (which can run over 10–20% of principal for subprime unsecured lenders) and the cost of capital, many lenders find that they need to charge triple-digit rates just to break even!

Financial Literacy Programs

Consumer advocates and the financial media are fond of lecturing Tight-ropers on what they should do and scorning them for what they actually do. They can often adopt a condescending position that people just need more financial education (or "financial literacy training" in the parlance of the industry) to make the "right" decisions with their money.

Education is never a bad thing, but it is not a silver bullet for the pressures of Tightropers. After reviewing the studies on the effectiveness of financial literacy courses, Richard Thaler, the Nobel prize-winning behavioral economist, stated that "financial education is laudable, but not particularly helpful." He added that "those who receive it do not perform noticeably better when it comes to saving more...or avoiding ruinous debt." Most concerning, he determined that "those who need the help most seem to benefit the least."[4]

There's a good reason why Tightropers ignore the wagging fingers of well-meaning consumer advocates and legislators and why financial literacy training has such limited value. Tightropers are street-smart about money. In fact, it can be argued that Tightropers are actually more financially literate, disciplined, and focused compared to those with greater resources and deeper pockets.

Because they have to be. They don't have any room for error.

According to research from the Center for the New Middle Class, Tightropers check their bank account balances 50% more frequently than the Safely Stable. They also check their credit scores 40% more than the Safely Stable.

Tightropers track their cash much closer than non-Tightropers and understand the concepts of budgeting and saving. They don't need budgeting worksheets. They don't need to be reminded of the envelope system of spending, saving, and giving. They don't need to be told that high interest rates are expensive. What they do need is more (and better) financial tools and options.

It's one thing to know how to budget and save. It's another thing to have a stable income and predictable expenses that enable regular, uninterrupted savings.

Unfettered Deregulation

If the political left reflexively gravitates to clamping down on lending options as the best way to aid Tightropers, the political right often goes too far in the opposite direction by supporting unfettered deregulation. Minimal accountability and oversight are just as potentially damaging as overly strict limits. The predictable result is abuse by unethical lenders.

Here's how quickly reform can go off the rails when the political extremes wrestle for control of common-sense regulation.

In 2017, the Consumer Financial Protection Bureau proposed a series of policy changes for small-dollar, short-term lending that would have limited the number of times a consumer could roll over a payday loan, required lenders to verify the ability of borrowers to reasonably repay their loans, and reduced the number of times a lender could attempt to draw payments from a customer's bank account. I was part of the bipartisan team (which included industry representatives as well as consumer advocates) that advised the CFPB on these rules and felt them to be very reasonable and balanced. They would have preserved access to credit but eliminated some very real abuses in the small-dollar lending industry.

Industry groups and their supporters in the media and Congress went ballistic in response to the proposed rules, even bringing legal action against the CFPB. And under the influence of the Republican administration, the proposed rules were ultimately shelved. As a result, legislators in some left-leaning states countered with harsh rate caps that dramatically reduced access to nonprime credit in their states.

Certainly, federal and state regulators need to be very cautious about the dangers of excessive regulations that can increase costs and limit the availability of credit. Earlier I mentioned the state attorney general who thought that panhandling was an acceptable alternative to credit for Tightropers. This cavalier and heartless view is why regulators need to worry about unintended consequences that can harm the people they are tasked to protect.

However, there are more than 100 million Tightropers in this country and they deserve improved protections against credit products that are not suited to their needs or that have the potential for significant financial harm in case of default. We shouldn't let politics imperil this important regulatory role.

...and Other Silly Stuff

Just one more bad idea to mention—Post Office banking. Recently, this idea has gotten traction as an answer to the proliferation of payday lenders across the US. The recommendation is that the Post Office provide short-term loans to consumers at very low interest rates.

Given that the Post Office currently loses billions every year on its core services, the idea that they will be able to provide banking services is ludicrous. Underwriting, servicing, and collecting on credit to Tightropers is extremely challenging and requires ongoing investment and innovation to stay current. It's hard to imagine that the Post Office will do so in an efficient manner. Furthermore, as we have detailed, Tightropers are already unhappy with the speed and convenience of service they receive at banks. Based on my experiences in recent visits to my nearby post office, I don't expect that Tightropers will find the staff and service levels at postal banks any friendlier or faster-paced.

To his credit, the former Postmaster General went on record stating that this is a bad idea. Unlike the proponents of this expansion of postal services, he understood the challenges that are inherent in providing credit. "People can very quickly say things like, 'Well, there's a lot of money to be made on service fees,'" Patrick Donahoe, the then-Postmaster General, told *American Banker* in a 2014 interview. "But a lot of the service fees in that world are based on high risk levels."[5]

Do we really want the American taxpayer to assume those risks?

19

OPPORTUNITIES FOR PRIVATE SECTOR INNOVATION

Making Tightropers a priority for investment

- It's time to unleash a new generation of financial products to help Tightropers.
- Innovators can make a positive impact while building lasting businesses.
- Silicon Valley needs to understand and invest in this massive opportunity.
- Employers will also need to rethink their assumptions on work and workers.

The primary institutions that serve our country—our banking system, our education system, and our healthcare system—are failing a growing percentage of Americans.

Tightropers are hardly unique in being frustrated with the current situation. Does anyone—no matter their economic situation—really think that banks, public schools and universities, and the healthcare system are doing a fantastic job? They all seem designed for a slower, less customer-focused era. Bankers still believe that customers have time to stand in long lines for service, schools and universities still focus as much on the needs of the faculty as the outcomes of students, and hospitals and medical offices still seem to spend more time pushing paper than caring for patients.

The good news is that this country has a thriving entrepreneurial spirit and investors and venture capitalists who are willing to fund bold and unproven ideas. Technology innovators have disrupted industry after industry, leading to lower costs, improved convenience, and fewer hassles. Not to mention just being cooler than the stodgy old offerings.

The government has a critical role to play in improving the financial health of Tightropers, but real innovation only comes from a focused private sector that sees opportunities to do things better, steal market share, and generate shareholder value.

I hope this book has convinced readers of the importance of improving the financial health of Tightropers in this country as well as the massive business opportunity they represent. Given that there are more than 100 million deeply underserved Tightropers, why haven't they become a visible focus of capital investment?

The dirty little secret of the venture capital community is that too often they think all customers are just like them. There have been a number of high-profile, venture-backed start-ups whose stated vision was to use advanced analytics to provide improved credit products to the "underserved." However, the founders often define their target "underserved" market as recent graduates from Ivy League schools who've just been hired into high-paying jobs in the technology industry. This niche focus on the well-educated and upwardly mobile doesn't begin to address the vast and growing need for financial services oriented to the needs of the average American Tightroper.

By listening to the stories of Tightropers and gaining an appreciation of their resilience and ideals, as well as their economic challenges, innovators and entrepreneurs can bring a new generation of products and services to market. These offerings will need to be designed around the real-world needs and concerns of Tightropers as a whole, not just the ones who look like Silicon Valley technologists and investors.

Here are some opportunities for innovators and private sector leaders who want to make a difference in the lives of Tightropers and build strong, differentiated businesses.

Give Tightropers the Credit (and Scores) They Deserve

It should come as no surprise that I am convinced of the need and opportunity for improved credit offerings designed specifically for Tightropers. Emergency credit products are essential to Tightropers and help them manage through uncertain financial times.

For the Safely Stable, credit providers compete aggressively with each other on rate, rewards, and convenience. However, credit products available to Tightropers are typically high cost, use aggressive collections, and often carry the risk of lost collateral such as a car or even a home. In fact, when talking to a potential investor in a previous business, I was told that the investment community expected nonbank lenders to have "obscene profits" based on aggressive collections.

As an entrepreneur, would you rather fight for market share in the world of "prime" credit—which is characterized by razor-thin margins and high customer acquisition costs—or go after the larger and less competitive market for "nonprime" credit?

Successful credit products for Tightropers must deliver a fast, hassle-free application experience, rapid funding, and extremely flexible options for customers who may struggle with on-time payments over the life of the loan. These are exactly the sort of things that Fintech innovators do best.

Furthermore, unlike most payday lenders, title lenders, and pawn lenders, Fintech disrupters are not saddled with branch locations and can provide credit through a wide variety of customer channels. Like the rest of us, Tightropers would prefer to apply and get funded for credit through their mobile devices rather than driving to a storefront location.

However, why wait for the customer to apply for credit at all? Fintech lenders have become increasingly integrated into the point of sale systems of merchants and service providers to pre-approve consumers for credit at the exact time they need it most. **Affirm**, **GreenSky**, **Klarna**, and others already do this for customers with excellent credit—Tightropers need an "Affirm for the Rest of Us."

It won't be enough, however, to compete exclusively on convenience and ease of application. Credit products for Tightropers must have certain features that don't matter to the Safely Stable. Since Tightropers are more likely to fall behind on their loan payments, they will need many of the features of Safety Net Credit that have been covered in this book. In the same way that Netflix conquered the DVD rental market by eliminating late charges, the upstart innovators who ultimately dominate the market for Tightroper credit won't rely on punitive fees. Instead, they'll offer payment flexibility and forbearance without judgment or embarrassment when customers experience job loss or other financial setbacks.

Underwriting Tightropers—Beyond FICO

The fact that banks don't serve Tightropers and that most nonprime credit products have extremely high rates of interest isn't due exclusively to ignorance or greed. Tightropers are more unstable, have higher loss rates, and are fundamentally more difficult to underwrite. As a result, most lenders make up for poor credit decisions by aggressively collecting against accounts that go past due.

The answer is better analytics, not tougher collections.

Serving Tightropers is challenging due to inadequacies in the credit data and analytics used for most underwriting decisions. Banks and other lenders still rely almost exclusively on information and credit scores provided by the "big three" credit bureaus (e.g., TransUnion, Experian, and Equifax) to determine creditworthiness.

Aaron Klein, the policy director of the Center on Regulation and Markets at the Brookings Institute, uses the analogy of the oboe in an orchestra to describe why credit scores like the well-known FICO score are so prevalent. "Do you know what instrument orchestras use for tuning before a performance? It's the oboe," says Aaron. "Not because it plays a true A. Quite the opposite. The oboe is actually the hardest instrument to tune. But it's better for all of the other instruments to match it—even if out of tune—rather than having all the other instruments in tune and the oboe playing flat.

"Because the entire financial system is tuned to FICO scores, nobody appreciates how deeply out of tune it is," suggests Aaron. As a result, improving FICO scores or even moving away from the use of FICO scores is extremely slow and difficult.

Some have recommended that additional information such as utility payment history should be added to credit scores or that alternate data such as social media posts could improve underwriting. Unfortunately, my experience is that this data has only marginal value in determining risk.

Fortunately, there are better options for improving the accuracy of underwriting Tightropers. In the past few years, providers such as **Plaid**, **Yodlee**, and **Finicity** (among others) have made it easy to access customer bank account data. Once the customer gives their approval, lenders receive upwards of two years of detailed bank transaction data—showing every payment into the account as well as every expense out of it.

This type of data provides far deeper insights into the credit affordability of Tightropers than traditional credit scores. With this data, lenders can see the historical cash flow of the customer, what kind of income volatility they face, and how they have spent their money in the past. They can see both good behaviors (regular additions to savings) and bad (regular visits to casinos). By assessing the trends, volatility, and even character traits evident in bank transaction data, lenders can develop far more insightful and accurate scores to underwrite Tightropers and ensure improved outcomes.

In a world that worries about the impacts of future pandemics on credit, bank data can provide a much better assessment of the up-to-the-moment stability of income and the extent of financial resources for managing through uncertain economic times.

Disrupt Dangerous Credit

Responsible, hassle-free, Safety Net Credit products are game-changers for Tightropers. They can help deal with life's ups and downs. And they fit well with the fast-paced lifestyles of Tightropers balancing families and often multiple jobs.

However, other forms of credit can be downright dangerous for Tightropers. Their unstable incomes and frequent unexpected expenses mean that they will occasionally suffer from cash shortfalls. And when that happens, they may not be able to make their loan payments.

Falling behind on credit card payments results in annoying calls from collectors and can damage your credit score. But other forms of debt don't have such insignificant downsides.

If you fail to repay your student debt, your income could be garnished and tax refunds and federal benefit payments withheld. Student debt loan servicers can take borrowers to court and charge them court costs, collection fees, attorney's fees, and other costs associated with the collection process. Your school may even withhold your academic transcript![1]

This situation is even worse when Tightropers have trouble with mortgage payments. They can end up homeless.

As has been highlighted earlier in this book, some Fintech upstarts are finding ways to provide equity-like financial products to replace these dangerous credit products. We need more of these innovations.

Income Share Agreements (ISAs) have the potential to help Tightroper students (and their parents) avoid taking on massive debt to attend the college of their dreams. They should be the first choice for Tightropers but unfortunately are not widely offered or understood. Industry leaders will need to do a much better job of communicating the benefits and making it just as easy to apply for and receive an ISA as a student loan (if not easier!).

ISAs should also be used for a broader set of educational expenses than traditional college. In fact, some programs that aren't eligible for federal student loans such as "coding boot camps" are beginning to use them. In some of these programs, such as at the Flatiron School, students can choose to pay 10% of gross income for four years after graduating but if their income falls under $40,000 annually, they will owe nothing.[2]

The concept of an Income Share Agreement has potential even outside of education. Many jobs these days require employees to move to a new town. How about ISA products to help people pay for moving expenses and start-up costs related to the new job?

Similarly, financial innovators need to provide better home ownership options for Tightropers than a traditional mortgage. Why not co-invest with Tightropers so that they can acquire housing without a down payment and without getting saddled with a 30-year mortgage? Investing in the house alongside the homeowner could minimize downside risk to the buyer while giving the investor upside appreciation potential without home maintenance costs.

Given the near-zero APRs on mortgages right now, I'm not sure I would recommend this for a Safely Stable customer with a high credit score. However, for a Tightroper, this sort of product is far better suited to their financial needs.

For aging Tightropers, these products can provide even more potential benefits. Reverse mortgages and home equity loans—not to mention 401(k) loans—can be financially devastating for our most at-risk Americans who can fall prey to aggressive sales pitches. They have a special need for new, less dangerous options for providing liquidity on their existing home investment.

These examples are just the tip of the iceberg for non-debt financial instruments that help Tightropers afford large expenses without the danger inherent in traditional credit products. Innovators need to continue to expand on the concept of swapping debt for equity in support of Tightroper stability and security.

Automate Financial Management and Advice

In today's fast-changing economy, Tightropers find that they need to supplement traditional jobs with "side hustles" to keep afloat. Yet at the same time they are increasingly stuck with more fixed expenses than ever before. Cell phones, internet access, streaming video services, and the like all have shifted from billing based on usage to fixed monthly charges. This is extremely convenient, but makes it very difficult to reduce expenses when income drops.

Even worse, as Tightropers receive more of their income from 1099 sources (that is, as contractors and part-time workers) than from W-2 sources (such as full-time employment), they need to account for tax liabilities and try to manage savings without automatic deductions and 401(k) savings plans. This means that Tightropers must have the discipline to put money into savings and not touch it to avoid later problems with tax authorities. We need to make it easier for Tightropers to focus on building their careers and financial success, not looking over their shoulder to make sure they don't inadvertently put themselves in a financial bind.

Challenger banks have proved that people will give control over their financial accounts to start-ups. **Chime**, **Dave**, and others have acquired millions of accounts in the past couple of years. Given the level of distrust that Tightropers have for traditional banks, there has never been a better time to raise our ambitions for Fintech innovation to improve financial management and advice.

Financial innovators need to start with accounts that are a better fit for Tightropers. They need to provide lots of constant updates (optimally via a mobile app) on spending, savings, and upcoming expenses (including taxes) so that Tightropers have more visibility and control over their rapidly changing financial situations.

Today, Tightropers are often surprised by overdrafts and late fees on bills they forgot to pay. In fact, I recently noticed that an applicant for credit with my company had experienced twenty-seven overdraft charges in the past thirty days! This person and millions like him deserve tools that "have his back" and prevent these unanticipated fees and expenses.

Furthermore, when Tightropers run short of cash during the month, they shouldn't be at risk of late fees on their rent payments (or worse, eviction). Instead, automated financial tools linked to emergency credit lines can ensure there are funds for expected payments and be able to step in to cover them when cash reserves run low.

With artificial intelligence, it is finally possible to provide the sort of financial coaching that Tightropers need but often can't afford. "Robo-advisors" tuned to the unique requirements of cash-constrained Americans can help Tightropers save money and avoid unnecessary charges.

Robo-advisors can also help Tightropers spend less. It is well-known that customers with less savings are often the ones paying the most for services like cell phones, internet access, insurance, etc. My experience analyzing Tightroper bank account behavior suggests that more than 50% are paying above market rates for their mobile plans. As we saw with products like **Truebill** and **Billshark**, once they are given access to customer bank accounts, these automated apps can function like a 24–7 financial advocate that is constantly trying to help them lower expenses and save money.

What should be clear is how foundational access to bank account transaction information is to these innovation opportunities for Tightropers. Only a few years ago Tightropers would have had to move their primary banking relationships to a new provider to give them this sort of access. Now, however, Tightropers can provide access to their data and innovators can mine it on behalf of their customers with just a click of a button. This has taken the friction away from Fintech innovation and opened the door to a new generation of powerful apps to help Tightropers improve their financial well-being.

Using access to bank data, for instance, automated financial management apps can automatically sweep money into the customer's account to help them avoid overdraft charges. This is a huge win for many Tightropers since an overdraft has an effective APR of 3,500% according to the FDIC (almost ten times higher than a payday loan!).

Similarly, automated financial management apps can leverage bank data to know when customers are about to make a regular payment such as rent or utilities. They can help customers avoid late charges and loss of service by reminding them of the upcoming payment and offering to pay it for the customers if needed.

The wealthy can afford a team of advisors who can look out for their financial interests, deal with unexpected expenses, and help them save for comfortable retirements. Technology innovation has the potential to democratize these services and make them available to the people who actually need them most: Tightropers.

Help Tightropers Monetize Their Data

The rise of social media represents the most remarkable transfer of wealth from "Labor" to "Capital" in history. Now people spend their time creating content to be shown by social media companies who then monetize it themselves. It is essentially the same thing as if people went to work in factories for fun and let the owners sell all of the goods that were created with no compensation.

Social media isn't the only offender. Credit bureaus and other data aggregators also profit from customer data that is rightfully the customer's to determine what to do with.

At a working session with other Fintech entrepreneurs sponsored by a leading hedge fund, one of the managing partners made an off-hand

comment that I thought was brilliant. He predicted that some bold entrepreneur would take on all of the lead aggregators and credit bureaus by
offering customers 90% of all of the revenue they made selling their data.
Most of the people in the audience laughed this off, but I think his idea
has real merit.

Since the average Tightroper has less than $400 in emergency savings,
even limited additional cash flows can help them avoid borrowing or selling personal property. We need to help Tightropers monetize their own
information and transfer that wealth back from Big Marketers and Big
Technology.

I expect that in the coming years we will see a new breed of data aggregators who are sensitive to this and realize how disruptive this could be.
For instance, wouldn't people move from Facebook to a similar provider
who paid them for their posts? And wouldn't we all like to be paid when-
ever a lender used our credit data to decide whether to offer us credit?
And if a lender was willing to pay $200 to get your application data sent
over from a lead generator, shouldn't you get a cut?

Transform the Workforce and the Workplace

The Gig Economy is the new reality in this country—especially for young
Tightropers. Even what seem like steady jobs can quickly evaporate in this
era of global competition and rapid technology changes that can make
jobs obsolete overnight.

Tightropers have no problem with "lifelong learning." We need employers to commit to this as well. They need to invest in ongoing training
for existing and new employees to help them keep their skills up to date
and they need to give workers the time to do this. It shouldn't be purely
the responsibility of the employee.

We also need improved online training programs to support lifelong
learning. Today's online training and certification programs are typically
either not realistic enough to substitute for actual on-the-job experience
or are extremely expensive. There is no reason we should accept either of
these situations. More sophisticated online and A.I.-based training

programs can do a much better job of simulating on-the-job challenges—even teamwork activities.

As we've discussed, however, this will require a sea change in the way most companies look to outside certifications. Today, far too many jobs require a traditional college degree (even if it's not actually required for the job), and most prioritize actual job experience over training. This makes it extremely hard for workers to transition to new jobs in a rapidly changing world. Employers need to invest in new approaches to help workers be nimble enough to cope with today's job insecurity.

The workplace itself also needs to change. The old assumptions of "nine-to-five" working hours in traditional office settings are being torn apart by the difficulties Tightropers face as they balance work and family obligations. In order to attract and retain talent, employers need to leverage technology to create more flexible and supportive work environments for the busy, challenging lives of their Tightroper employees.

Prior to COVID-19, the general assumption was that employees needed to be at their desks to be productive and contribute to their teams. Now, the rapid transition to Zoom meetings and virtual interactions has proven this unnecessary.

Tightropers—like it or not—are the future of our workforce. We need to rethink all aspects of the workplace to support their needs and help them be productive and successful.

I'VE BUILT SUCCESSFUL businesses serving Tightropers over the past 20 years. However, given the vast number of Tightropers in this country (not to mention globally) and the urgency of their unmet needs, my modest efforts have only scratched the surface. I predict that some of the most profitable and valuable companies built in the next two decades will be focused on serving and transforming the financial lives of Tightropers.

20

BUSINESS IDEAS THAT DON'T WORK

Failed innovations and dead-end ideas

- Innovators need to avoid paternalistic approaches.
- Unprofitable concepts don't help—Tightropers don't want charity and they don't trust products that seem "too good to be true."
- Silicon Valley innovators have an opportunity to make a difference in the lives of Tightropers if they listen and learn.

N ot all of the approaches favored by Silicon Valley entrepreneurs for serving Tightropers are based on a deep understanding of the consumer and their real-world situation. Many companies have opted for paternalistic approaches and others treat Tightropers as victims in need of saving. These don't work. The following are some of the flawed approaches for serving Tightropers that should be avoided:

Gamification and Nudging

Books by and about the famous social behavioralist, Richard Thaler, and his peers created a tremendous amount of excitement in certain circles. The idea that we can "trick" people into doing the right things with their lives has appeal to people who think Tightropers face financial stress due to mistakes and bad decisions.

There were a number of companies and products launched with the idea that social nudging and providing "badges" for good behavior could engineer improved outcomes. Unfortunately, I am not aware of any meaningful successes.

Nor am I personally exempt from criticism in this area. I was excited about the potential of gamification and structured one of our credit products to reward people for a wide variety of behaviors (from on-time payments to taking financial literacy programs). Rather than leading to happy customers with lower rates and higher repayment rates, customers found the process complicated and off-putting. Ultimately, we simplified things dramatically to almost universal thanks.

Tightropers, like all of us, are extremely suspect of and resistant to manipulation. And given how many of them have been taken advantage of by service providers, who can blame them? Products serving Tightropers must be particularly respectful and transparent to avoid frustration and resentment.

Friction

One thing that can doom many products designed for Tightropers is "friction." What I mean by this are the well-intentioned barriers that companies put in place, intending to help the customer.

For instance, a Fintech company launched a product to provide very low-cost credit to people with damaged credit scores as long as they could get several friends or relatives to "vouch" for the customer and agree to chip in money if they didn't repay the debt. While an interesting idea, the product didn't take into account the urgency at which Tightropers need access to emergency credit. They don't have the time (or inclination) to ask friends for help—they have too much pride for that. The company eventually folded.

Another component of friction is high rejection rates. A number of start-ups have attempted to use Big Data analytics to identify the small percentage of Tightropers that will perform like people with prime credit scores. However, by design they decline the majority of applicants. Aaron Klein at the Brookings Institute warns lenders to be careful about the "psychic pain" that a potential credit decline has for consumers. "I think that's why a lot of people keep sticking with the payday lenders," he surmised. "They are aware that there are better products out there, but at least the payday lender will approve them with no hassles."

Companies that provide services to Tightropers need to understand how busy they are and how much their time (and dignity) means to them. They have families to support, they often work multiple jobs, and, of course, they want to have rich personal lives. They don't have time to waste—even to save some money. Products and services need to be designed with this lifestyle in mind.

Giveaways

Today, there are a remarkable number of extremely valuable companies that seem like they will never make money. Uber, Lyft, AirBnB, WeWork, etc. are all examples of big bets that were made assuming the companies would eventually be able to charge more for their services and/or build the scale suitable for long-term profitability.

Numerous financial service companies have been launched under this business model. They provide bank services with no fees and hope that somehow they will be able to make money where banks can't.

Tightropers are nearly as suspicious of deals that sound "too good" as they are of deals that seem abusive—and they should be. Uncertainty is the killer for Tightropers. They want service providers who are stable and have strong business models that will endure for the long-term.

The Challenge for Silicon Valley

How has the Silicon Valley technology community so completely missed out on the massive market potential posed by the rapid growth of Tightropers in America? Although financial technology firms have been a hotbed of start-up investments in the past decade, they have largely competed to provide credit and other financial services for the 1%—the ones already swimming in low-priced, traditional credit options.

Silicon Valley influencers and decision makers need to wake up to the new financial reality facing this country.

The goal of this book is to increase awareness of the challenges facing so many Americans and to highlight the opportunities that wait for those who commit to making a difference. It's exciting to imagine the kind of improvements that technology innovation can make in the lives of Tightropers and their families once business leaders start listening to their stories.

21

THE TIME TO ACT IS NOW!

Throughout this book, you've seen data on the perilous financial lives of millions of American Tightropers. You've seen how difficult it has become to build a financial safety net and to save for retirement. You've read about how each stage of life brings new obstacles to stability and new challenges that can push people off of the Tightrope. And you've seen how the traditional prescriptions for success and the traditional institutions in this country are failing so many hardworking people.

More importantly, you've heard the stories of Tightropers themselves. You've learned about their lives, their resilience, and their deep commitments to their families and their communities.

Tightropers know the way forward.

Will the rest of us listen?

In this highly polarized political environment, we gravitate toward traditional policy recommendations from the "right" and "left" rather than fresh thinking that challenges outdated approaches. This sort of confirmation bias threatens our ability to respond to changing economic realities and make a lasting impact.

If we don't take our cues from the lived experiences of Tightropers themselves, the much-derided cycles will continue. Policy battles will yield no significant change. Lenders and regulators will continue their comfortable pattern of mutual demonization. And entrepreneurs and investors will never realize the opportunity that Tightropers represent for industry disruption and innovation.

The impact of rising financial insecurity—especially in the wake of COVID-19—is the most critical economic challenge facing this country. If we don't respond to the changes that have created so many American Tightropers, we will see a generational shift toward disenfranchisement and frustration. And we will not be able to afford to support them as they age and prepare for retirement, creating even more hardships for families trying to do the right thing.

We all have a part to play.

Policymakers and Legislators

Common ground is increasingly rare these days, but we need to commit to new state and federal programs that help Tightropers build savings for emergencies as well as retirement—and prevent them from being drained.

Policymakers and legislators need to stop pointing fingers and wishing the world could go back to stable times. The economic pressures that created Tightropers are here to stay and we need new policy initiatives to address them. We need recognition that steady income is increasingly rare and that the majority of Americans may come to rely on the gig economy to provide for their families.

Fortunately, we don't need a vast restructuring of the social fabric to make a difference. Instead, we need to focus on programs that give more financial control to Tightropers and create stronger incentives to help them build their own safety nets. Tightropers are capable and hard-working—they need programs and policies that help them build for their future in this age of instability.

Regulators

Outdated regulatory perspectives on the financial risk of lending to Tightropers hold banks back from serving the average American and have driven people to nonbank products such as payday loans and title loans.

Regulators need to stop being so focused on interest rates as the sole determinant of whether a financial product is "responsible." Instead, they should be more concerned with the potential downsides from default and how to encourage lenders to offer Safety Net Credit products that provide flexibility and forbearance for customers when they face financial setbacks.

Most importantly, regulators need to ensure that banks, as well as non-bank lenders, start saying "yes" to mainstream American Tightropers who need financial support.

Bankers

Banks have incredible competitive advantages. They receive essentially free cost of capital and they don't have to follow the complex and often bizarre state-by-state lending laws. Furthermore, they have the financial backing of the federal government.

As a result, it should be absolutely unacceptable to us as taxpayers that they don't effectively serve the emerging financial needs of Tightropers— the fastest growing economic segment of this country. We need bankers to make a new commitment to serve average Americans with products that fit their fast-paced lives, recognize their increasing levels of financial fragility, and don't punish them when they struggle to make payments.

Entrepreneurs, Innovators, and Investors

The biggest opportunity for business innovation and growth is right under our noses. Tightropers represent an enormous but misunderstood market. Entrepreneurs need to step outside of the 415 and 212 area codes and listen to Tightropers. They will help inform a new wave of technology-enabled financial tools and services and create millions of loyal and profitable customers.

Silicon Valley needs to recognize that the country is changing rapidly and that the average American doesn't go to college and doesn't have family and friends to lean on when times are tough. By learning directly from Tightropers and building products and services for their unique needs, innovators will find exciting new market opportunities with limited competitive challenges.

Educators

This book has made it clear that educators are failing Tightropers. The outcomes and risks of college enrollment are increasingly not worth the cost. However, Tightropers need education and training more than ever to succeed in the current fast-changing economy.

The fundamental changes that have been caused by the COVID-19 pandemic also bring unique opportunities to restructure education for the current financial realities facing Tightropers of all ages. We need to create lower-cost models of delivery and new sources of educational funding to reduce student debt. And we need to leverage technology to help Tightropers reskill quickly to keep up with an ever-changing world.

Employers

Flexibility is one of the most critical needs for Tightropers. Their lives change rapidly, and they are constantly forced to juggle the needs of family, work, and all of the daily issues that life throws at them.

Employers play an important role in helping to create a more supportive environment for Tightropers. Thanks to shelter-in-place orders across the country, we have learned that spending our days sitting in office cubicles is no longer a requirement for businesses to function effectively. Employers need to continue to expand their thinking on flexible work environments and support their employees dealing with ongoing pressures and disruptions. Furthermore, they need to commit to ongoing retraining to ensure lifelong growth and productivity for employees.

Tightropers Themselves

More than anything else, Tightropers need to keep telling their stories. We all need to hear from them about what works, what doesn't, and how we can come together as a nation to increase their financial stability and help them achieve improved long-term financial outcomes.

Regulators, businesspeople, policymakers, and academics must admit we haven't served Tightropers well. Instead of including and listening closely to Tightropers, we kept them at arm's length and continued to feed them outdated prescriptions for how to succeed. Even worse, we've provided paternalistic advice on how to deal with the fundamental economic changes that are impacting their lives.

Meanwhile, Tightropers keep on keeping on. In a system stacked against them, they keep figuring out their own way forward, even though many take one step back for every step forward.

Tightropers would make faster progress toward firmer ground if everybody else walked with them, as equals and peers. If politicians asked for their opinion rather than just their vote. If the media asked Tightropers for their recommendations, not just for their stories of frustration. If business leaders and financial entrepreneurs specifically included them in product development and marketing. If lenders and regulators talked with Tightropers as smart consumers instead of talking down to them.

Tightropers know the way forward. They'll get there on their own. How much better it would be for the rest of us if we walked with them.

ACKNOWLEDGMENTS

This book covers a lot of ground. It's not just about the need for financial innovation—a subject that I have a lot of direct experience with—it's also about the many stresses that have caused financial hardship for millions of Americans and the broad set of things that can make a positive difference in their lives.

Fortunately, I've been helped by an amazingly accomplished and thoughtful group of individuals. Jonathan Walker, who leads the Center for the New Middle Class, provided the data and stories that formed the basis for much of my thinking about how Tightropers differ from the Safely Stable. He has been invaluable to this project and probably knows more than anyone on the planet about how Tightropers manage their lives, having interviewed hundreds of them over the years. I also want to thank Ron Suber, Kathy Boden Holland, Aaron Klein, Bill Isaac, Tim Ranney, and Bob Johnson for their insights and friendship over the years. While they aren't to blame for any of the content in the book, without their help, the book would have had far less scope and ambition. And huge thanks to the absurdly talented Chance Harris for the cover concept and charts throughout the book.

Equally important to this book are the tireless efforts of the people I've worked with over the years at previous and current companies to innovate and constantly deliver better products and services. They pushed me to think past profits and focus on making a lasting difference in the lives of the Tightropers we served. Our mission—Good Today...Better Tomorrow—has never seemed more vital.

My coauthor, Joanne Cleaver, helped me shape and articulate the stories of Tightropers and encouraged me to rely less on numbers and charts and more on the human reality. She didn't realize it would be a multiyear engagement when we started this project and has been a terrific partner through it all.

Special thanks go to my Dad who read the entire manuscript not once but twice, making great recommendations each time. Definitely well above and beyond the call of duty.

My friend Anthony helped me connect theory with people. His life and accomplishments are an inspiration.

And of course, I wouldn't have finished without the support of my wife, Jeanne, who grew up a Tightroper and has never been discouraged when my business dealings risked making us Tightropers again.

ENDNOTES

Chapter 1

1. CareerBuilder, "Living Paycheck To Paycheck Is a Way of Life for Majority of U.S. Workers, According to New CareerBuilder Survey," press release, August 24, 2017 (Harris Poll conducted for CareerBuilder).
2. Board of Governors of the Federal Reserve System, "Report on Economic Well-Being of US Households" (Washington, DC: US Federal Reserve, 2019).
3. Diana Farrell and Fiona Greig, "Paychecks, Paydays, and the Online Platform Economy" (New York: JP Morgan Chase & Co. Institute, 2016).
4. Adrian D. Garcia, "Survey: Most Americans Wouldn't Cover a $1K Emergency with Savings," Bankrate Financial Security Index (January 2–6, 2019) https://www.bankrate.com/banking/savings/financial-security-january-2019.
5. CareerBuilder, "Living Paycheck To Paycheck."
6. Ethan Dornhelm, "US Average FICO Score Hits 700: A Milestone for Consumers," FICO (July 10, 2017). Kenneth P. Brevoort, Philipp Grimm, and Michelle Kambara, "Data Point: Credit Invisibles" (Washington, DC: CFPB Office of Research, May 2015).
7. "Payday Loans, Auto Title Loans, and High-Cost Installment Loans" (Washington, DC: CFPB Office of Research, June 2, 2016).
8. Ethan Dornhelm, "US Average FICO Score Hits 700." Brevoort, Grimm, and Kambara, "Data Point: Credit Invisibles." Jessica Semega, Kayla Fontenot, and Melissa Kollar, "Income and Poverty in the United States" (Washington, DC: US Census Bureau, September 2018). Spectrem Group, "Spectrem Group's 2019 Market Insights Report Reveals 10th Consecutive Annual Increase in Wealthy American Households," press release, March 12, 2019.
9. "United States Personal Savings Rate: 1959–2020," Trading Economics, accessed August 25, 2020, https://tradingeconomics.com/united-states/personal-savings.
10. Emmanuel Saez and Gabriel Zucman, "Wealth Inequality in the United States since 1913: Evidence from Capitalized Income Tax Data," *Quarterly Journal of Economics* 131, no. 2 (May 2016): 519–78. Elisabeth Jacobs and Jacob Hacker, "The Rising Instability of American Family Incomes, 1969–2004 Evidence

from the Panel Study of Income Dynamics" (Washington, DC: Economic Policy Institute, May 28, 2008).

11. David Harrison and Maureen Linke, "Historic Asset Boom Passes by Half of Families," *Wall Street Journal*, August 30, 2019.

12. Thomas Piketty, *Capital in the Twenty-First Century*, trans. Arthur Goldhammer (Cambridge, MA: Belknap Press of Harvard University Press, 2014).

13. David B. Muhlhausen, *Do Federal Social Programs Work?* (Santa Barbara, CA: Praeger, 2013).

14. Daniel Herbst, Henry S. Farber, Ilyana Kuziemko, and Suresh Naidu, "Unions and Inequality Over the Twentieth Century: New Evidence from Survey Data" (Cambridge, MA: National Bureau of Economic Research, May 2018): http://www.nber.org/papers/w24587.

15. Ben Bernanke, "The Real Effects of the Financial Crisis," BPEA Conference Drafts, (Washington, DC: The Brookings Institution, September 2018).

16. Timothy P. Carney, *Alienated America: Why Some Places Thrive While Others Collapse* (New York: Harper, 2019).

17. Martin Ford, *Rise of the Robots: Technology and the Threat of a Jobless Future* (New York: Basic Books, 2016).

18. Shawn M. Carter, "Social Media May Be Making You Overspend—And It's Not Just Because of the Ads," CNBC, March 15, 2018, https://www.cnbc.com/2018/03/15/social-media-may-make-you-overspend-and-its-not-just-because-of-ads.html.

19. Benjamin Kreider, "Risk Shift and the Gig Economy," *Working Economics* (blog) (Economic Policy Institute, August 4, 2015): https://www.epi.org/blog/risk-shift-and-the-gig-economy.

20. Jesse Colombo, "How Interest Rate Hikes Will Trigger the Next Financial Crisis," *Forbes*, September 27, 2018, https://www.forbes.com/sites/jessecolombo/2018/09/27/how-interest-rate-hikes-will-trigger-the-next-financial-crisis/#424ba1156717.

21. Kari Paul, "Young People Blame Climate Change for Their Small Retirement Accounts," *Barron's*, May 27, 2019, https://www.barrons.com/articles/millennials-saving-for-retirement-51558676997.

22. Elise Gould and Jessica Schieder, "Poverty Persists 50 Years After the Poor People's Campaign: Black Poverty Rates are More Than Twice as High as White Poverty Rates" (Washington, DC: Economic Policy Institute, May 17, 2018).

23. Jeffrey P. Thompson, Joanne W. Hsu, Lindsay Jacobs, Lisa J. Dettling, and Kevin B. Moore, with assistance from Elizabeth Llanes, "Recent Trends in Wealth-Holding by Race and Ethnicity: Evidence from the Survey of Consumer Finances" (Washington, DC: US Federal Reserve, September 27, 2017).

24. Jhacova Williams and Valerie Wilson, "Racial and Ethnic Income Gaps Persist Amid Uneven Growth in Household Incomes," *Working Economics* (blog) (Economic Policy Institute, September 11, 2019): https://www.epi.org/blog/racial-and-ethnic-income-gaps-persist-amid-uneven-growth-in-household-incomes/.

25. Center for the New Middle Class, "African American Financial Experience; Prime and Non-prime," Elevate, February 2018, https://www.newmiddleclass .org/wp-content/uploads/2019/12/African-American-financial-experience -Feb.-2018.pdf.

26. Melat Kassa and Zane Mokhiber, "By the Numbers: Income and Poverty, 2018," *Working Economics* (blog) (Economic Policy Institute, September 10, 2019): https://www.epi.org/blog/by-the-numbers-income-and-poverty-2018.

27. Center for the New Middle Class, "African American Financial Experience."

28. "Total Population by Child and Adult Populations in the United States," Kids Count Data Center, updated August 2019, https://datacenter.kidscount.org /data/tables/99-total-population-by-child-and-adult#detailed.

29. Ethan Dornhelm, "US Average FICO Score Hits 700."

30. Brevoort, Grimm, and Kambara, "Data Point: Credit Invisibles."

31. Semega, Fontenot, and Kollar, "Income and Poverty in the United States."

32. Spectrem Group, "Spectrem Group's 2019 Market Insights Report."

Chapter 2

1. The Tightropers you'll meet in this book are real people. Some of their stories come from conversations I've had with them, and some come from conversations or interactions with the staff at the Center for the New Middle Class. As is customary, identifying details, such as names and locations, have been changed, and they have been lightly edited, but the specifics of their situations are accurate and true.

2. Emmanuel Saez and Gabriel Zucman, "Wealth Inequality in the United States since 1913: Evidence from Capitalized Income Tax Data," *Quarterly Journal of Economics* 131, no. 2 (May 2016): 519–78.

3. CareerBuilder, "Living Paycheck To Paycheck Is a Way of Life for Majority of U.S. Workers, According to New CareerBuilder Survey," press release, August 24, 2017 (Harris Poll conducted for CareerBuilder).

4. Amanda Dixon, "Survey: Nearly 4 in 10 Americans Would Borrow Money To Cover a $1K Emergency," Bankrate, January 22, 2020, https://www.bankrate .com/banking/savings/financial-security-january-2020.

5. Center for the New Middle Class, "Non-prime Americans: The Scourge of Unexpected Expenses," Elevate, January 2017, https://www.newmiddleclass .org/non-prime-americans-the-scourge-of-unexpected-expenses.

6. Center for the New Middle Class, "Understanding the Drivers of Non-Prime Credit," Elevate (May 2019): https://www.newmiddleclass.org/understanding -the-drivers-of-non-prime-credit-may-2019.

7. Gina Martinez, "GoFundMe CEO: One-Third of Site's Donations Are to Cover Medical Costs," *Time*, January 30, 2019.

8. Center for the New Middle Class, "Limited Options for Borrowing: The Non-Prime Experience," Elevate, March 2017, https://www.newmiddleclass .org/limited-options-for-borrowing-the-non-prime-experience.

9. Elevate analysis from Elevate Prospectus, April 6, 2017, https://www.sec.gov /Archives/edgar/data/1651094/000119312517114348/d310075d424b4.

10. Ethan Dornhelm, "US Average FICO Score Hits 700: A Milestone for Consumers," FICO (July 10, 2017). Kenneth P. Brevoort, Philipp Grimm, and Michelle Kambara, "Data Point: Credit Invisibles" (Washington, DC: CFPB Office of Research, May 2015).

11. Center for the New Middle Class, "New Study: Credit Status correlates to Experiences with Dating," Elevate, February 2019, https://www.newmiddleclass .org/new-study-credit-status-correlates-to-experiences-with-dating-february -2019.

12. Center for the New Middle Class, "The Banking Experience: Prime vs. Non-Prime," Elevate, April 2018, https://www.newmiddleclass.org/the-banking -experience-prime-vs-non-prime-april-2018.

13. Center for the New Middle Class, "The Banking Experience: Prime vs. Non-Prime."

14. "FDIC Study of Bank Overdraft Programs" (Washington, DC: Federal Deposit Insurance Corporation, November 2008).

15. Center for the New Middle Class, "The Banking Experience: Prime vs. Non-Prime."

16. While it is true that subprime mortgage portfolios were a significant cause of the Great Recession, data published by TransUnion (Ryan Boyle and Ezra Becker, "Personal Loan Performance During Times of Stress," TransUnion, 2016) shows that subprime unsecured loan portfolios actually experienced a smaller percentage increase in losses during the Great Recession than prime and super-prime portfolios.

17. Elevate analysis from Elevate Prospectus, April 6, 2017, https://www.sec.gov /Archives/edgar/data/1651094/000119312517114348/d310075d424b4.

18. Lalita Clozel, "Otting Pushes Banks To Offer Payday Style Loans," Wall Street Journal, January 16, 2018.

19. "Payday Loans, Auto Title Loans, and High-Cost Installment Loans," CFPB.

20. "New Poll: 9 in 10 Payday Loan Borrowers Felt Product Met Their Expectations, Are Highly Satisfied and Value the Service," Community Financial Services Association of America, December 4, 2013, https://www.businesswire.com /news/home/20131204005905/en/New-Poll-9-10-Payday-Loan-Borrowers.

21. Donald P. Morgan and Michael R. Strain, "Payday Holiday: How Households Fare after Payday Credit Bans," Federal Reserve Bank of New York, Staff Reports Number 309, revised February 2008, https://www.newyorkfed.org /research/staff_reports/sr309.html.

22. "Complaint Snapshot: 50 State Report" (Washington, DC: Consumer Financial Protection Bureau, October 2018): https://files.consumerfinance.gov/f /documents/bcfp_50-state-report_complaint-snapshot_2018-10.pdf.

23. Alvaro Puig, "What You Should Know About Payday Loans and Car Title Loans" (Washington, DC: Federal Trade Commission, April 23, 2020): https://www.consumer.ftc.gov/blog/2020/04/what-you-should-know-about -payday-loans-and-car-title-loans.

24. "CFPB Finds One-in-Five Auto Title Loan Borrowers Have Vehicle Seized for Failing to Repay Debt" (Washington, DC: Consumer Finance Protection Bureau, May 18, 2016): https://files.consumerfinance.gov/f/documents/201605 _cfpb_single-payment-vehicle-title-lending.pdf.

Chapter 3

1. According to the Thomas Jefferson Foundation, this is a spurious quote. Whoever the author was, they understood an important aspect of our democracy.
2. All data and charts in this chapter were graciously provided by the Center for New Middle Class from an unpublished July 2019 study of the politics of prime and nonprime Americans. It was based on a survey of over 1,000 prime and nonprime Americans.
3. The survey took place shortly after the Equifax and Capital One data breaches.
4. The survey took place during a heat wave covering most of the US.

Chapter 4

1. Jasmine Kim, "Coronavirus Deaths in U.S. Projected To Surpass 200,000 by October," CNBC, June 17, 2020, https://www.cnbc.com/2020/06/17/coronavirus -deaths-in-us-projected-to-surpass-200000-by-october.html.
2. Charisse Jones, "Layoffs: 1.3M Workers File for Unemployment as COVID-19 Spikes and Businesses Close Again," *USA Today*, July 9, 2020.
3. Katherine Lucas McKay, Sam Gilman, and Zach Neumann, "20 Million Renters Are at Risk of Eviction; Policymakers Must Act Now to Mitigate Widespread Hardship," The Aspen Institute (June 19, 2020): https://www.aspeninstitute .org/blog-posts/20-million-renters-are-at-risk-of-eviction.
4. Danny Hougherty and Eric Morath, "Pandemic Employment: Winners and Losers," *Wall Street Journal*, July 11, 2020.
5. Center for the New Middle Class, "Non-Prime Tracker Report," Elevate (June 2020).
6. Center for the New Middle Class, "Non-Prime Tracker Report."
7. Maggie Fitzgerald, "U.S. Savings Rate Hits Record 33% as Coronavirus Causes Americans To Stockpile Cash, Curb Spending," CNBC, May 29, 2020, https://www.cnbc.com/2020/05/29/us-savings-rate-hits-record-33percent -as-coronavirus-causes-americans-to-stockpile-cash-curb-spending.html.
8. "The Early Effects of the COVID-19 Pandemic on Credit Applications" (Washington, DC: Consumer Finance Protection Bureau, April 2020): https://files .consumerfinance.gov/f/documents/cfpb_issue-brief_early-effects-covid-19 -credit-applications_2020-04.pdf.
9. Center for the New Middle Class, "Non-Prime Tracker Report."
10. "The $2 trillion CARES Act, a response to COVID-19, is equivalent to 45% of all 2019 federal spending," USAFacts, April 5, 2020, https://usafacts.org

/articles/what-will-cares-act-and-other-congressional-coronavirus-bills-do
-how-big-are-they.

11. James V. Grimaldi, "Nation's Top Emergency Preparedness Agency Focused
on Warfare Threats Over Pandemic," *Wall Street Journal*, July 9, 2020.

12. Lorie Konish, "About $1.4 billion in stimulus checks sent to deceased Ameri-
cans," CNBC, June 25, 2020, https://www.cnbc.com/2020/06/25/1point4
-billion-in-stimulus-checks-sent-to-deceased-individuals.html.

13. Fred Imbert, "Treasury Secretary Mnuchin Says It Was 'Outrageous' for the
LA Lakers To Take a Small Business Loan," CNBC, April 28, 2020, https://
www.cnbc.com/2020/04/28/mnuchin-says-it-was-outrageous-for-the
-lakers-other-such-businesses-to-take-small-business-loans.html.

14. "Considering an Early Retirement Withdrawal? CARES Act Rules and What
You Should Know," *Consumer Finance Protection Bureau* (blog), June 2020.

15. Center for the New Middle Class, "Non-Prime Tracker Report."

Chapter 5

1. Emma Kerr and Melissa Shin, "See High School Graduation Rates By State,"
US News and World Report, April 22, 2020.

2. "Immediate College Enrollment Rate," (Washington, DC: Institute of Education Sciences at the National Center for Education Statistics, April 2020).

3. Tom Allison, "Financial Health of Young America: Measuring Generational De-
clines between Baby Boomers and Millennials," Young Invincibles Federal Reserve Study, January 2017, https://younginvincibles.org/wp-content/uploads
/2017/04/FHYA-Final2017-1-1.pdf.

4. Tom Allison, "Financial Health of Young America."

5. Social Security and Medicare Boards of Trustees, "A Summary of the 2020
Annual Reports" (Washington, DC: Social Security Administration, 2020).

6. Richard Eisenberg, "How to Fix Social Security for Vulnerable Americans,"
Forbes, July 5, 2018.

7. Kim Parker, Rich Morin, and Juliana Menasce Horowitz, "Retirement, Social
Security and Long-term Care," Pew Research Center, Social and Demographic
Trends, March 21, 2019.

8. Andrew Van Dam, "The Unluckiest Generation in U.S. History," *Washington
Post*, May 27, 2020.

9. Andrew Dunn, Eric Wilson, Katy Golvala, and Thea Garon, "U.S. Financial
Health Pulse: 2018 Baseline Survey Results" (Chicago: Financial Health Network, 2018): https://s3.amazonaws.com/cfsi-innovation-files-2018/wp
-content/uploads/2019/05/07151007/FHN-Pulse_Baseline_SurveyResults
-web.pdf.

10. "Early Adulthood: The Pursuit of Financial Independence," (New York: Merrill Lynch and Age Wave, 2019): https://mlaem.fs.ml.com/content/dam
/ML/Registration/merr9555_EarlyAdulthoodStudy_v05a_pages.pdf.

11. Dunn, Wilson, Golvala, and Garon, "U.S. Financial Health Pulse."

Chapter 6

1. Mark Kantrowitz, "A Look at the Shocking Student Loan Debt Statistics for 2020," Student Loan Hero, January 15, 2020. Available at https://studentloan hero.com/student-loan-debt-statistics.
2. A. Dundar, F. Huie, Y. A. Hwang, A. Nathan, D. Shapiro, P. Wakhungu, and X. Yuan, "Completing College: A National View of Student Attainment Rates by Race and Ethnicity—Fall 2010 Cohort," National Student Clearinghouse Research Center, Signature Report No. 12b, April 2017.
3. Phil Izzo, "Congratulations to Class of 2014, Most Indebted Ever," *Wall Street Journal*, May 16, 2014, https://blogs.wsj.com/numbers/congatulations-to-class -of-2014-the-most-indebted-ever-1368.
4. National Education Association, "Average Teacher Salary Down 4.5 Percent, NEA Report Finds," Press Release, April 29, 2019, http://www.nea.org/home /44479.htm.
5. Hillary Hoffower, "Nearly Half of Indebted Millennials Say College Wasn't Worth It, and the Reason Why Is Obvious," *Business Insider*, April 11, 2019.
6. Douglas Webber, "Is College Worth It? Going Beyond Averages," Third Way, September 18, 2018.
7. Center for the New Middle Class, "College Tuition: How Non-prime Families Cover College Tuition," Elevate, August 2018, https://www.newmiddleclass .org/college-tuition-how-non-prime-families-cover-college-tuition.
8. Complete College America, https://completecollege.org.
9. Zack Friedman, "Student Loan Debt Statistics in 2018: A $1.5 Trillion Crisis," *Forbes*, June 13, 2018.
10. Liz Knueven "College Is More Expensive Than Ever, But 'Almost No One' Is Paying Sticker Price," *Business Insider*, September 16, 2019.
11. Judith Scott-Clayton, "The Looming Student Loan Default Crisis Is Worse Than We Thought," (Washington, DC: The Brookings Institution, January 11, 2018): https://www.brookings.edu/research/the-looming-student-loan -default-crisis-is-worse-than-we-thought.
12. Cherone Duggan, "Could College Be Free?" *Harvard Magazine*, January/February 2020.
13. Michael Stratford, "How Bernie Sanders Would Cancel All Student Loan Debt," *Politico*, June 24, 2019.
14. Jason Delisle, "Should We Forgive All Federal Student-Loan Debt?" *Wall Street Journal*, May 27, 2020.
15. Archie Hall, "Shares in Students: Nifty Finance or Indentured Servitude?" *Financial Times*, November 11, 2019.
16. Archie Hall, "Shares in Students."
17. Texas Department of Licensing and Regulation, Cosmetology, updated August 5, 2020, https://www.tdlr.texas.gov/cosmet/cosmet.htm.
18. Heather Lalley, "Chipotle Expands Its Tuition Assistance Program," *Restaurant Business Magazine*, October 15, 2019.

19. Mary Jo DiLonardo, "'Signing Day' Recognizes High School Seniors Starting Jobs, Not College," Tree Hugger, April 11, 2019, https://www.treehugger.com /signing-day-recognizes-high-school-seniors-starting-jobs-not-college-4863319.

Chapter 7

1. "The Deloitte Global Millennial Survey 2019," (London: Deloitte, 2019): https://www2.deloitte.com/content/dam/Deloitte/global/Documents /About-Deloitte/deloitte-2019-millennial-survey.pdf.
2. "The Deloitte Global Millennial Survey 2019."
3. Jonathan Rothwell, "Earning Income on the Side Is a Large and Growing Slice of American Life," *New York Times*, December 18, 2019.

Chapter 8

1. Richard Fry, "It's Becoming More Common for Young Adults To Live at Home—and for Longer Stretches" (Washington, DC: Pew Research Center, May 5, 2017).
2. Bhargavi Ganesh, Jun Zhu, Jung Choi, Laurie Goodman, and Sarah Strochak, "Millennial Homeownership—Why Is It So Low, and How Can We Increase It?" (Washington, DC: Urban Institute, July 2018): https://www.urban.org /sites/default/files/publication/98729/millennial_homeownership_0.pdf.
3. "Boomerang Generation, Returning to the Nest," TD Ameritrade, May 2019, https://s2.q4cdn.com/437609071/files/doc_news/research/2019/Boomerang -Generation-Returning-to-the-Nest.pdf.
4. Irina Lupa, "The Decade in Housing Trends: High-Earning Renters, High-End Apartments and Thriving Construction," *RentCafe* (blog), December 2019, https://www.rentcafe.com/blog/rental-market/market-snapshots/renting -america-housing-changed-past-decade.
5. Sydney Temple, "America's 2018 Rental Market in Review: Renters Finally Get Relief," Abodo, January 1, 2019, https://www.abodo.com/blog/2018-annual -rent-report.
6. The Economic and Housing Research Group, "A Steadily Growing Housing Market," Freddie Mac, May 15, 2019.
7. "United States Core Inflation Rates (1957–2020)," US Inflation Calculator. https://www.usinflationcalculator.com/inflation/united-states-core-inflation -rates.
8. Alex Gray, "Still living with your parents? You're Not Alone," *World Economic Forum*, November 11, 2016, https://www.weforum.org/agenda/2016/11/why -do-so-many-young-adults-still-live-with-their-parents-in-these-countries.
9. Niall McCarthy, "Report: 81% Of Young Italians Still Live With Their Parents," *Forbes*, October 25, 2016, https://www.forbes.com/sites/niallmccarthy/2016

/10/25/report-81-of-young-italians-still-live-with-their-parents-infographic
/?sh=17b2e6eb36fa.

Chapter 9

1. Carol Graham and Julia Ruiz Pozuelo, "Happiness, Stress, and Age: How the U-Curve Varies across People and Places," *Journal of Population Economics* (August 2016): https://www.brookings.edu/wp-content/uploads/2016/08/global _20160825_happiness_stress_age.pdf.

Chapter 10

1. Kevin Kuczynski, Marc Lino, Nestor Rodriguez, and TusaRebecca Schap, "Expenditures on Children by Families, 2015" (Washington, DC: United States Department of Agriculture, March 2017): https://fns-prod.azureedge.net /sites/default/files/crc2015_March2017_0.pdf.
2. Lena Rizkallah, S. Katherine Roy, and Sharon Carson, "Guide to Retirement," JP Morgan Asset Management 2016, https://am.jpmorgan.com/blob-gim /1383280097558/83456/JP-GTR.pdf.
3. "Employment Characteristics of Families Summary" (Washington, DC: US Bureau of Labor Statistics, April 21, 2020): https://www.bls.gov/news.release /famee.nr0.htm.
4. Kuczynski, Lino, Rodriguez, and Schap, "Expenditures on Children by Families, 2015."
5. Elizabeth Warren and Amanda Warren Tyagi, *The Two-Income Trap: Why Middle-Class Parents are Still Going Broke* (New York: Basic Books, 2004).
6. Christina Caron, "The Costly Burden of Day Care and Preschool," *New York Times*, April 17, 2020.
7. Carlie Berke, "Divorce With Children: How Much Does It Cost and How Long Does It Take?" YourMoneyAdvocate, August 9, 2018, https://yourmoney advocate.net/divorce-with-children-how-much-does-it-cost-and-how-long -does-it-take/.
8. Adam Looney and Vivien Lee, "Parents Are Borrowing More and More To Send Their Kids To College—and Many Are Struggling To Repay" (Washington, DC: The Brookings Institute, November 27, 2018): https://www.brookings .edu/research/parents-are-borrowing-more-and-more-to-send-their-kids -to-college-and-many-are-struggling-to-repay/
9. Brady Porche, "Poll: 3 in 4 Parents with Adult Kids Help Them Pay Debts, Living Expenses," Creditcards.com, December 11, 2017.
10. Jesse Noyes, "7 Big Statistics About the State of Flexible Work Arrangements," Zenefits, July 11, 2018.
11. "Employment Characteristics of Families Summary," (Washington, DC: US Bureau of Labor Statistics, April 21, 2020).

12. "The Cost of Childcare" (Washington, DC: Economic Policy Institute, July 2019): https://www.epi.org/how-does-your-state-stack-up-annual-infant-care-costs.
13. Nicole Lyn Pesce, "How Some Coworking Spaces Are Disrupting the Child Care Industry," MarketWatch, December 17, 2018.
14. Melia Robinson, "The 'Uber for Childcare' Lets Parents Order a Nanny through an App," *Business Insider,* January 27, 2016.

Chapter 11

1. Gary Koenig, Lori Trawinski, and Sara Rix, "The Long Road Back: Struggling to Find Work after Unemployment" (Washington, DC: AARP Public Policy Institute, March, 2015): https://www.aarp.org/content/dam/aarp/ppi/2015-03/struggling-to-find-work-after-unemployment.pdf.
2. Melanie Curtan, "Attention, Millennials: The Average Entrepreneur Is This Old When They Launch Their First Startup," *Inc.*, May 17, 2018.

Chapter 12

1. Jessica Dickler, "What Americans Really Want for the Holidays Is To Pay Down Debt," CNBC, November 19, 2019, https://www.cnbc.com/2019/11/19/paying-down-debt-tops-the-holiday-wish-list-for-many-americans.html. Board of Governors of the Federal Reserve System, "Consumer Credit Outstanding (Levels)" (Washington, DC: US Federal Reserve, August 7, 2020): https://www.federalreserve.gov/releases/g19/HIST/cc_hist_mt_levels.html.
2. "Planning and Progress Study 2018," Northwestern Mutual 2018, https://news.northwesternmutual.com/planning-and-progress-2018.
3. Joe Resendiz, "Average Credit Card Debt in America: 2018," ValuePenguin by LendingTree, August 18. 2020, https://www.valuepenguin.com/average-credit-card-debt.

Chapter 13

1. "Planning and Progress Study 2018," Northwestern Mutual.
2. "Planning and Progress Study 2018," Northwestern Mutual.

Chapter 14

1. Christine Benz, "75 Must-Know Statistics About Long-Term Care: 2018 Edition," Morningstar, August 20, 2018, https://www.morningstar.com/articles/879494/75-must-know-statistics-about-long-term-care-2018-edition.

2. Jane Gross, "Elder-Care Costs Deplete Savings of a Generation," *New York Times*, December 30, 2006.

3. Benz, "75 Must-Know Statistics About Long-Term Care."

4. Benz, "75 Must-Know Statistics About Long-Term Care."

5. Grace Gedye, "The Strange Political Silence on Elder Care," *Washington Monthly*, July/August 2019.

6. Benz, "75 Must-Know Statistics About Long-Term Care."

7. Benz, "75 Must-Know Statistics About Long-Term Care."

8. "The MetLife Study of Caregiving Costs to Working Caregivers: Double Jeopardy for Baby Boomers Caring for Their Parents," MetLife, 2011, https://www .caregiving.org/wp-content/uploads/2011/06/mmi-caregiving-costs-working -caregivers.pdf.

9. Benz, "75 Must-Know Statistics About Long-Term Care."

10. Howard Gleckman, *Caring for Our Parents: Inspiring Stories of Families Seeking New Solutions to America's Most Urgent Health Crisis.* (New York: St. Martin's Press, 2009).

11. "Elderly Population," OECD, Accessed on 23 August 2020, https://data.oecd. org/pop/elderly-population.htm.

Chapter 15

1. "TIAA-CREF Survey: Nearly One-Third of Americans Have Taken Out A Loan from Their Retirement Plan Savings," TIAA-CREF, June 18, 2014, https:// www.tiaa.org/public/about-tiaa/news-press/press-releases/pressrelease505 .html.

2. Jean A. Young, Olivia S. Mitchell, Stephen P. Utkus, and Timothy (Jun) Lu, "Borrowing From the Future: 401(K) Plan Loans and Loan Defaults," (Cambridge, MA: National Bureau of Economic Research, April 2015): https:// www.nber.org/papers/w21102.pdf.

Chapter 16

1. Ari Houser, Lynn Friss Feinberg, Molly Evans, Rita Choula, and Susan Reinhard, "Valuing the Invaluable 2019 Update: Charting a Path Forward," AARP Public Policy Institute, November 2019.

2. Bob Pisani, "America's Retirement Accounts Are Growing, But Not Fast Enough," June 12, 2019. CNBC, June 12, 2019, https://www.cnbc.com /2019/06/12/americas-retirement-accounts-are-growing-but-not-fast-enough .html.

Chapter 17

1. Jacob S. Hacker, "The Economy Is Strong. So Why Do So Many Americans Still Feel at Risk?" *New York Times*, May 21, 2019.
2. "The 401(k) Participation Rate Is Shocking," Financial Samurai, updated in 2019, https://www.financialsamurai.com/the-401k-participation-rate.
3. Ezra Becker and Ryan Boyle, "Personal Loan Performance During Times of Stress," TransUnion, 2016.
4. Ken Rees and William M. Isaac, "Regulators Can Help American Workers Get the Credit They Deserve," *Wall Street Journal*, October 26, 2017.

Chapter 18

1. Josh Mitchell, "The Long Road to the Student Debt Crisis," *Wall Street Journal*, June 7, 2019.
2. "Out-of-pocket spending," Peterson Center on Healthcare-KFF Health System Tracker, available at https://www.healthsystemtracker.org/indicator/access-affordability/out-of-pocket-spending.
3. Ann Carrns, "An Alternative to Payday Loans, But It's Still High Cost," *New York Times*, September 21, 2018.
4. Richard H. Thaler, "Financial Literacy, Beyond the Classroom," *New York Times*, October 5, 2013.
5. Kevin Wack, "Postal Banking Is Back on the Table. Here's Why That Matters," *American Banker*, April 26, 2018.

Chapter 19

1. "Student Loan Delinquency and Default," Federal Student Aid, an Office of the US Department of Education, https://studentaid.gov/manage-loans/default.
2. Kevin Carey, "New Kind of Student Loan Gains Major Support. Is There a Downside?" *New York Times*, December 16, 2019, https://www.nytimes.com/2019/12/16/upshot/student-loan-debt-devos.html.

ABOUT THE AUTHOR

KEN REES is a financial technology innovator who is passionate about serving the underserved. Over the past two decades he has founded and grown multiple companies, launched numerous financial products, and served millions of American "Tightropers."

Ken is founder and CEO of Covered, a disruptive Fintech dedicated to providing affordable healthcare financing to people who struggle with less-than-prime credit scores. Before that, he was founder and CEO of Elevate, a leading online lender that he took public on the New York Stock Exchange. Additionally, he was the founder and CEO of CashWorks, a financial technology company acquired by GE.

He is a frequent speaker and writer on financial technology and financial inclusion topics and has been profiled in the *New York Times* and his opinion pieces have appeared in the *Wall Street Journal, American Banker,* and *Business Insider* among other publications.

In 2012, Ken was selected by Ernst & Young as an Entrepreneur of the Year and was named a 2017 Innovator to Watch by *Bank Innovation.*

He lives in San Francisco, CA with his wife and dog.